T0294341

WALKING THE VALLEYS

WALKING THE VALLEYS

Urban walks in the Cynon, Rhondda, Rhymney & Taff valleys

Peter Finch & John Briggs

SEREN

is the book imprint of
Poetry Wales Press Ltd.
Suite 6, 4 Derwen Road, Bridgend,
Wales, CF31 1LH

www.serenbooks.com
facebook.com/SerenBooks
twitter: @SerenBooks

© Peter Finch, 2022
Photographs © John Briggs, 2022

The right of Peter Finch to be identified
as the author of this work has been asserted
in accordance with the Copyright,
Designs and Patents Act, 1988.

ISBN 978-1-78172-686-0

A CIP record for this title is available
from the British Library.

All rights reserved.
No part of this publication may be
reproduced, stored in a retrieval system,
or transmitted at any time
or by any means electronic,
mechanical, photocopying, recording
or otherwise without the prior permission
of the copyright holders.

The publisher works with the financial
assistance of the Books Council of Wales.

Cover photograph: Malcolm Robertson's *Pit Heads* in Hanbury Square, Bargoed.

Printed by Severn, Gloucester.

CONTENTS

Alun Lewis –
Mountain Over Aberdare

HOW TO USE THIS BOOK

The walks in this book are all located in the four main valleys that lead, in one way or another, to Cardiff – the Rhondda, the Taff, the Cynon and the Rhymney. Some are linear, most are circular. They are walks largely for the urban explorer rather than the long distance walker. At the time of writing they all follow legal and accessible routes. Trespass on to private land might offer short cuts but these are not recommended. Decent shoes and some rain protection are minimum requirements.

Route descriptions offer plenty for the armchair walker. Maps are provided as are web links to Plotaroute, an online route planner at www.plotaroute.com where the precise routes followed have been recreated enabling walkers to check their progress against ours on their phones. For basic desktop usage this service is free but for as little as £18 you can access the enhanced *Premium* version which offers mobile use plus a whole range of other benefits. OS maps are best followed using the survey's own proprietary software at www.ordnancesurvey.co.uk/shop/mapfinder which can render both Landranger and Explorer maps in high resolution. There is a charge for this service.

Ynysmeurig Road, Abercynon

INTRODUCTION

In this bright corner of south east Wales there are two places you need to know about. They are utterly inter-dependent and are permanently connected, although sometimes you wouldn't think so. The one is a rich, diverse, and cosmopolitan capital; the other a spread of ribbon dormitories. They fill the space between the city's northern border and the Brecon Beacon's southern edge. Cardiff and the Valleys.

Every day thousands of valley residents travel to the city for work in the capital's service industries, call centres, company administrations and government offices. They stream down the rail lines that once carried coal and along the roads built over the once revolutionary canal. They spend leisure time and money in the city's clubs, restaurants, stores, cinemas, cultural institutions and bars. On big rugby days the national stadium will be filled with their chanting. Their accents have played a big part in the cutting zing of Cardiff's own, mixing in with Irish brogue and West Country burr. This town is theirs. They belong here. Cardiff and the Valleys are two parts of the same place.

Cardiffians themselves, however, sometimes take a different view, if they take a view at all. The Valleys, they imagine, are distant disenfranchised places. They rarely visit. The nearest valley involvement many city dwellers get will be a glimpse of the slate-roofed terraces from the window of a car speeding up the A470, heading for the English Midlands or points north. When shown a map many Cardiffians would not be able to point to Porth, Bargoed or Rhymney with any certainty. For them the city is the place.

Over the decades what was to become the capital sucked its hinterland dry of resource, cash and talent creating what has been called American Wales: an un-Welsh wonderland that provided everything its population needed. Why would Cardiffians want to visit the coal black snake-bend upper reaches of the Taff or the runs of pits squashed into every available place along the whole defile of the Rhondda? Over its one hundred and fifty or so years of history, that difference between capital and hinterland has done nothing but grow.

Once coal had ceased to be the desirable product it had originally been and had started instead to acquire the qualities of eco disaster, attitudes began to change. City dwellers, some of them, now wanted to discover where and how the coal had been won. Less easy now that everything including the river waters had been cleaned. But not impossible. A few sets of winding gear remain at Big Pit, Tower, Lewis Merthyr, Penallta and Hetty Pit at Hopkinstown. Here are museums at Rhondda Heritage Park, Big Pit and at New Tredegar. There are also other traces of the past. The chapels, the reading rooms and the miners' institutes, closed mostly and in decay but not yet all demolished. There are the terraces, the valley-side steps that teeter upwards so steeply that it's as if they are reaching for heaven. There are the cafés, the pubs, and there are, of course, the people. Valley residents who greet you as an old friend even if they've just met you and are always willing to talk, endlessly it often seems, about absolutely anything.

Penallta Colliery headgear

In the rush to rid the Valleys of all memory of what had developed them in the first place tips have been removed, surface buildings flattened, washeries demolished, pit head baths converted to apartment housing and transport links lifted or permanently changed. In some places today it is almost as if industry had never existed. These towns are country villages set in hilly ground. Or might have been mistaken as such if it were not for the business parks built on their outskirts and the corrugations of their endless terraces.

The industrial revolution had, to put it mildly, a dramatic effect on Wales. The total population in the mid-eighteenth century, just before the rush to make iron followed by the unadulterated stampede to dig coal, was only around 500,000. By the nineteen-twenties when the steam-powered explosion had reached its peak it had risen to 2,600,000.

Terraced Housing, Porth

That was a geometric increase and an enormous number of these new arrivals found their way onto the housing terraces and into the ever-deepening coal pits of the south Wales Valleys.

The driver initially had been the money to be made working in the never more than a few miles wide iron belt that ran from Dowlais to Clydach. This had been followed by immigration to the much larger and much more significant coalfield which covered the entire south-east like the print from a giant's thumb.

Coal was the fuel of the age. Although initially the main customer for the products of the pits were the iron furnaces which used coal for smelting, it was the invention of the steam engine that significantly increased consumption. Suddenly the world ran on steam. Trains, ships, mills, lorries, factories. Consumption was enormous. The new industrial workers' houses were all coal heated. The pits themselves burned coal in order to power their pit wheels. While all this industry writhed the skies were permanently dark.

The valleys run north-south. They spread out across south Wales like an expanding fan. There are eight in total. Or seven. Or twenty-one. Interpretations differ. They fill the land from Carmarthen to Monmouth with their defiles.

All have at some stage had truck with coal extraction. And for most this became a heroically transformational activity that changed their rural natures forever. Even today with coal long gone and many of its waste tips flattened the housing stock and the transport links remain.

The first valley residents brought non-conformist practices with them. The place they were moving to lacked any kind of civic tradition so a new one had to be created. New arrivals based society on the pit, the chapel and on the union. They created their own cultural institutions, and relied enormously on their fellow workers for support. By their nature residents were independent-minded and rebellious. The society they founded was close knit and self-reliant. Valley communities became sacred things.

Valleys are named after their rivers or the towns at their heads. The big coal extractions took place in the Merthyr, the Cynon, the Rhondda and the Rhymney and while some used the docks at Barry and Penarth for their exports the majority of the coal went through Cardiff. The capital even committed the unforgivable sin of stealing Newport's bounty by manipulating the Rhymney Railway so that it pointed its coal trucks at Cardiff rather than Newport.

Today valley habitations are still essentially villages with a few, Porth, Pontypridd, Bargoed, large enough to be called towns. Merthyr, the biggest, has applied for city status although quite what benefit that would bring remains unclear.

Bargoed High Street

Work is a scarce commodity. Housing stock is poor and has low occupation. This is particularly the case towards valley tops. Proposals have been made to demolish a lot of the poorer properties here and to refurbish and reshape what remains. This would give valley communities new purpose, help them develop green industries and new tourism. A well-funded programme of regeneration would offer hope. As ever, controversy hovers. Why should money be spent here? Why do the inhabitants continue to reside in small, unserviced northern valley towns? Why don't they move south where housing is better and work more readily available? Why should they, is a common response.

In valley towns there is usually little flat ground. The centre, near the river and where a modicum of space is available has normally been given over to the settlement's reason for being there: the colliery and its associated workings. Housing clusters in zigzag rows up the valley sides. Built at impossible angles with access roads steeper than any present day planning regulation would ever allow. Where rivers meet and there's what in Welsh is known as an aber or an ystrad there the town can sprawl a little. This is how we get the wonders of Ystrad Mynach, Abercynon and Aberdare. But mostly it's impossible hillside construction and that's the joy.

In *Walking The Valleys* the photographer John Briggs and I have taken a look at the central south Wales Valleys – those big operators: the Rhondda, the Cynon, the Rhymney and the Merthyr (or the Taff, as it often known). These are ones that the world knows. They are sources for that singing Welsh accent, for coal, humour, blackened faces, strikes, and pit disasters. They appear in a plethora of twentieth century literary works, tv dramas and Hollywood films. John and I wanted to see how much remained and to attempt, on behalf of the larger non-valley population, some demystification.

Do not expect day-long valley to valley tours or confluences with nature and meditations on the power of the skies (although there might be a touch). These walks are mostly our introductions to the valley landscape, its industrial and earlier history, its psychogeography and, as a real bonus, its cafés and its people. Expect tea you can stand spoons in and toast as thick as your wrist.

Our approach has been consistent. Research, visit, research again, revisit and do that as many times as seems necessary.

Walk the patch slowly. Talk to those you meet. Check out what you've heard. John's celebrated and instinctive approach to photography has been a triumph. His unerring ability to capture the Valleys essence and to involve both its people and its landscape works every time.

On occasion we've recruited companions who know the patch to show us around. Dai Smith did this in Tonypandy. Daryl Leeworthy took us around Pontypridd. The poet Mike Jenkins walked us through Merthyr. Elsewhere we've asked, looked and read up.

Walks are arranged alphabetically with the exception of Merthyr Tydfil. Merthyr's dominance of the northern end of the valleys, as a town beyond them, is unique. It was the centre of the Welsh industrial revolution, home of the earliest ironworks and the first great pits, and for a time the largest town in Wales. Merthyr was simultaneously a town apart and valleys' centre. With its unique history and plethora of extant artifacts, buildings and historical places John and I spent a lot of time here. We've given it pride of place as the culmination of our valley walks.

We start and finish each individual walk at a railway station. This discipline will make access easy and with engaging views from train windows as you travel nothing less than worthwhile. It does mean, though, that where the rail operators have seen fit to lift tracks, to Maerdy for example, or Tredegar, then significant components of Valley history have been missed. A volume two, by bus, may well sort that out.

"Cardiff shall be famous when the sun goes down" wrote Idris Davies in *Gwalia Deserta* in 1938. But for a daytime excursion try coming here to the Valleys.

THE ROUTES

Abercynon	2.77 miles	https://www.plotaroute.com/route/1011471
Aberdare	4.50 miles	https://www.plotaroute.com/route/813051
Aberfan	4.32 miles	https://www.plotaroute.com/route/1718549
Bargoed	2.74 miles	https://www.plotaroute.com/route/1038750
Caerphilly	4.80 miles	https://www.plotaroute.com/route/916056
Gelli	4.33 miles	https://www.plotaroute.com/route/955821
Gelligaer	6.45 miles	https://www.plotaroute.com/route/1658108
Pontypridd	3.36 miles	https://www.plotaroute.com/route/973398
Porth	2.81 miles	https://www.plotaroute.com/route/1000026
Rhymney	4.63 miles	https://www.plotaroute.com/route/1647381
Taff's Well	3.24 miles	https://www.plotaroute.com/route/1022154
Tonypandy	4.48 miles	https://www.plotaroute.com/route/877222
Treherbert	4.34 miles	https://www.plotaroute.com/route/1081221
Ystrad Mynach	6.86 miles	https://www.plotaroute.com/route/1653455
Merthyr	5.88 miles	https://www.plotaroute.com/route/1748022

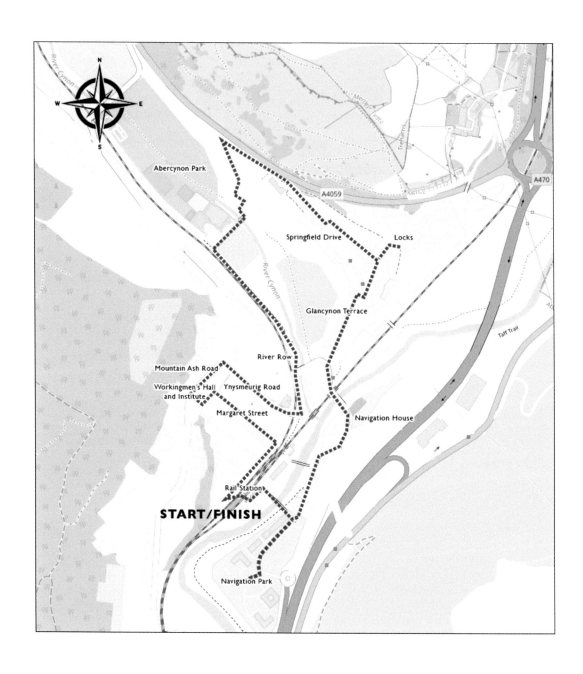

ABERCYNON

2.77 miles.
www.plotaroute.com/route/1011471

In times before anyone began making iron in quantity in that thin strip of land at the heads of the Valleys this place was a farm or two and a cottage. It was known as Ynysmeurig if it was known as anything. The Meurig part came from twelfth century Ifor ap Meurig, Lord of Senghenydd, stormer of Cardiff Castle and consummate Welsh hero. Senghenydd is just over the mountain, Mynydd Eglwysilan, from here. And Ifor Bach, as ap Meurig was commonly known, now has a club named after him in Womanby Street, in the Welsh heart of Cardiff. Here in Abercynon rivers met, the Taff and the Cynon, thrashing together at a spot called Watersmeet. They are as clear again today as they were when Ifor forded them.

Things began to change, as they did across most of the Valleys landscape, towards the end of the eighteenth century. This was when the iron that had been made near Merthyr since at least Roman times was turned into a vast fire breathing and landscape-demolishing industry by Thomas Lewis and Isaac Wilkinson. The pair established a works at Dowlais Brook in 1759. Near at hand were supplies of iron ore, coal, limestone, wood and water: all the ingredients necessary. Their project was a success and the idea spread. The iron ingots produced right across the heads of the Valleys were exported through the ports at Cardiff and Newport. They travelled at first by slow pack horse, then by tramway-fed canal, and finally by the Taff Vale Railway. All these transport thoroughfares met at Abercynon.

The Glamorgan Canal climbing down dozens of locks reached Watersmeet in 1792. The branch from Aberdare got here in 1812. Ynysmeurig morphed from farmland backwater to buzzing hub. The place became known, successively, as Aberdare Junction, Navigation, and Y Basin. None of these names really worked. A public meeting held in 1893 came up instead with the name Abercynon[1].

The rail station we arrive at is, by Valley Line standards, large and well equipped. It's been the recipient of EU funding and is complete with a graffiti-free pedestrian underpass wide enough to drive a Volkswagen through. There's a plaque above the entrance to railway trade unionist

John Ewington, fueller of the strike which led to the founding of the Labour Party. Here the red wall hangs on.

We head west, crossing the newly created and somewhat underused stretch of Park and Ride tarmac between the rail-tracks and the river. This is the combined river now, Taff and Cynon flooding south together. The bridge takes us directly to Navigation Park, a latter-day business park job creation project of the kind ubiquitous on the sites of former collieries throughout the Valleys. This one sits over what was once the huge Abercynon Colliery that, at its height in 1924, employed 2802 men. The shaft had been sunk in 1889 to provide coking coal for the new Dowlais Cardiff steelworks. At the time it was the deepest pit in the coalfield. It blackened the landscape with dust and tip waste until it closed in 1988. Abercynon author George Ewart Evans reports seeing these tips sliding well before the tragedy of Aberfan.

We stroll past bright new brick, carpark-surrounded enterprises which offer the expected mix of environmental, telecommunications, software, graphics, road haulage, security, business management and training services. The Valleys Innovation Centre. Things you can't quite put your finger on but guess you know what they are. Nothing dug, nothing made, nothing much physically created here anymore. At the centre stands a seven ton Pennant sandstone block faced with bronze bass reliefs depicting miners at work. This is John Allinson's 1995 Abercynon Colliery Memorial sited more or less where the pit shaft went down.

We retrace our steps between parked Volvos and men dressed as salespeople talking intently on their phones to exit along River Court heading north towards Navigation House. If anything stands for Abercynon then it is this structure. Readily visible to travellers on both the nearby A470 and the Taff Trail this building is now an inn. It was formerly the headquarters of the Glamorgan Canal Company and, for a time, the largest iron exchange in the world. Built in 1792 as an hotel it changed function many times to finally become the Celtic Carvery in 2012. It outlives any physical sign of the many wharfs, basins, barges and loads of iron ingots and coal that once poured through this node.

Beyond it, running under the council offices and the local fire station, was the Penydarren Tramroad along which the very first passenger-carrying steam-hauled train journey in the world occurred. The tramroad, along which horse-hauled trucks of iron made their way down from Merthyr, was used for the settling of a 500 guinea wager between the perpetually argumentative and difficult Merthyr Ironmaster Richard Crawshay and his litigious rival, Samuel Homfray, owner of the Penydarren Works. The wager was that Cornish engineer Richard Trevithick's steam engine recently built at Penydarren could pull 10 tons of iron and 70 passengers the sixteen kilometres down from the ironworks to the canal at Navigation. Unaided and under steam. Note the word 'down' there. Homfray was clearly onto a winner. It could, and, despite having to temporarily dismantle its funnel in order to pass through a tunnel, it did. Although the engine gave up the ghost trying to manage the incline empty on the way back and had to be hauled home by horse.

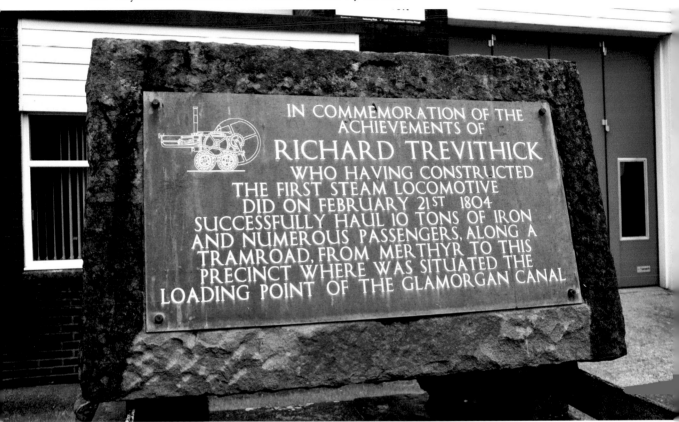

Claims are often made that the first steam train journey was made along the Stockton and Darlington Railway by Locomotion No 1 built by George Stephenson. The National Rail Museum at York, which houses that engine, is often at the forefront such suggestions. But Locomotion's trip was in 1825. Trevithick's engine made its journey in 1804.

In the nineteen-eighties the National Museum of Wales built a working replica of the great engine. They used Trevithick's original drawings and as near as they could constructed it of similar materials. It ran once a month on Steam Sunday outside the Industrial and Maritime Museum at Cardiff Docks. Today it sits, no longer functioning but eminently viewable, at that Museum's reincarnation as the Waterfront Museum in Swansea.

If you are not Welsh then being Cornish comes a pretty close second, although from a Welsh perspective it might have been better if Trevithick had actually been called

Thomas, but there you go. The local authority have celebrated his achievement by the creation of the way-marked Trevithick Trail. This runs for nine miles to the north of here doubling as the Taff Trail to Penydarren in Merthyr. It's a worthy diversion if you have the time but we miss it. Instead we cross back across the Cynon again to reach what the road signs grandly call Abercynon (West).

Here Cardiff Road becomes Glancynon Terrace at the place where the largest chapel in the Cynon Valley, Calfaria, once stood. Ewart Evans describes this as "looming up like a cliff" next to the grocer's shop at Bristol House which his father owned. The chapel was demolished in 1983 and a block of sheltered flats built on the site.

The Evans family shop is still there though, albeit reconstructed as a Premier Convenience store. The Rhys Davies Trust has installed a memorial slate plaque above the door. George Ewart Evans was not your regular Valleys Welsh author. He rose to fame by almost single-handedly developing the art of field recording ordinary working-class people. He was a sort of Welsh version of American blues and folk song collectors Alan and John Lomax but specialising in talk rather than song. He moved to East Anglia and wrote his best seller *Ask The Fellows Who Cut the Hay*, a cornucopia of reportage from the swiftly vanishing rural world. If he'd stayed in Abercynon that book might have been very different. Beyond the pit streets and the industrial devastation he reckoned the middle ages still existed out there on the Welsh hills.

Glancynon Terrace gives way to Argyll Street as we climb slowly up the valley side. Turning right at the street sign indicating 1,2 & 4 Dock Cottages we reach a place of vanished power, a psychogeographer's dream where what was absolutely no longer is. This is the precise spot where the Aberdare Canal joined the one that came down from Merthyr. A junction to mirror that of the local rivers. There was a basin, a wharf, a barge repair operation, and a run of cottages. Gone. The land now given over to a few bushes and a rough place where you can three-point turn a car.

At the end of Springfield Drive, to the side of Plymouth House, are the remains of one of the stairway of sixteen locks that brought the Glamorgan Canal down the hillside. Further lock stonework fills the back garden where landscaping has blended neat flower borders, a summerhouse and garden statuary deftly into the industrial remains. Not quite as

CADW would do it but the locks still exist and there is evidence of repointing of the stonework and restoring the sides. The predecessor to Plymouth House, the lock keeper's cottage here at the junction, sat on a sort of island, surrounded by canal and feeder on all four sides.

Leaving, we head north-west along Fife Street and then Greenfield Terrace. This is the start of the Cynon Valley proper and the route of the canal to Aberdare. Most of it has now been lost under the roaring A4059. The houses have a studied, settled nature about them. Their porches are filled with buddhas, concrete statuary of figures in hats, owls, dogs, birds, stone flowers. Green Men, loads of those. Beyond the school, Ysgol Gynradd Abercynon, we go back on ourselves, downhill towards Valley bottom and the green expanse of the allotments and Abercynon Park.

A Cynon river bridge takes us past the sports centre to join the Cynon Trail, which passes the Green Valley Centre's Community Greenspace. Here volunteer Mike Jenkins and his helpers are developing a biodiverse and very green facility for the use of locals. There are beehives, ponds, recently planted hazel coppices and huts and sculptures made from woven reed and willow. There's a dragon too but that more resembles a large dog than anything that could breathe fire. A Celtic garden, one visitor described it. Despite the future being uncertain as futures often are, we are given the tour with huge enthusiasm. The place is a gem.

Further along we enter the terraces of River Row, tiny, two-bed, stone-built workers' cottages threatened by heavy passing traffic, mining subsidence, and river flood. The one boarded For Sale looks as if it might be one we could buy, should we ever want to do that. John reckons the cottages here would go for fifty but when I check later the cheapest turns out to be almost double at £80K. Abercynon, a place rising in the world[2].

Ducking under the rail bridge with Watersmeet behind us we enter Abercynon Central, the beating heart, the mining village. The route zig zags through the streets, climbing Ynysmeurig Road past the combined town war memorial and clock, crossing along Mountain Ash Road and then descending Margaret Street. The steepness takes me by surprise having told myself that like, for example, Bargoed in the Rhymney, this Valley is not the Rhondda so it'll be a stroll in the park. The pull up is every bit as hard as the worst in Clydach Vale or Ferndale.

Ynysybwl   4
B 4273

Mountain Ash
Aberpennar   4
B 4275

46

Abercynon, terraced streets and stairs

From the top at Mountain Ash Road the whole of the valley is spread out and I am struck by how much hillside stands bare and how seemingly underdeveloped this whole townscape now looks. Immediately below us is the vacant buddleia and bramble filled site of what was the largest Workingmen's Hall and Institute in this district. Built in 1904 the main hall could accommodate 1700 with several further hundred in a subsidiary space. Being built on a hillside it was thirty-five feet high at the rear but a full seventy at the front. At street level it had cafés and general stores. It was demolished in 1994 as too expensive to maintain. Another speck of irreplaceable valley history swept into the wind.

At the seaside-themed Jellyfish Café at the top of Margaret Street we get builder's tea and white-bread toast done to perfection. The run of stores here hang on by their teeth. A chippy. Pizza parlour. Mortgage and loans operation. Hairdresser. Barber. Loosemore's Royal Dutch Chocolate Café. Charity shop. Bob & James Tools, with a handwritten door notice warning NO LARGE GROUPS OF PEOPLE AT ONE TIME IN SHOP PLEASE. No sunbed operators, no phone shop and, as far as I can see, no pawnbroker, not yet.

Returning to the train we pass David Dower Close, a memorial to the flyweight champion boxer and former collier, Dai Dower (1933-2016) who was born nearby. The lanes between the runs of houses are grass green. The train service back to the big city is unrivalled. Because Abercynon is on both the line to Merthyr Tydfil and the one to Aberdare it gets a city bound two-car Transport for Wales (TfW) train every fifteen minutes.

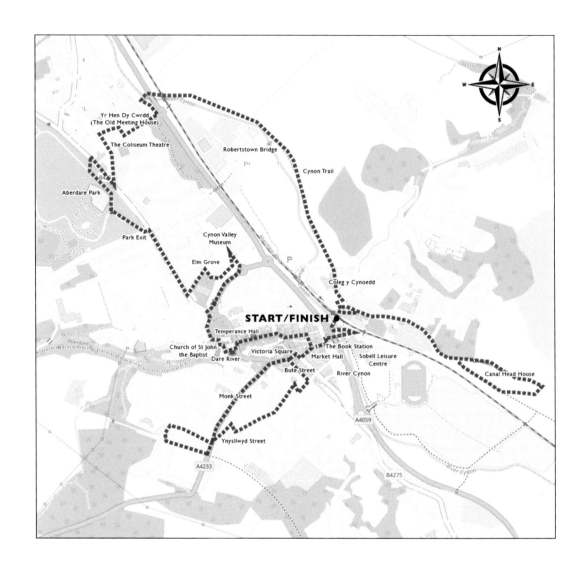

ABERDARE

4.50 miles
www.plotaroute.com/route/813051

Aberdare, the Queen of the Valleys, is like Rome. The remains of history, or memorials to it, lie everywhere on its surface. Is this an exaggeration? Sure. But for a place in south east Wales this one hangs on to much more of its past than many do. Its earlier history is that of a market town built at the aber[3] where the Dare River joins the Cynon, and centred on the squat church of St John the Baptist. A Christian outpost among the grazed fields and places where mills turned slowly. But like everywhere else in these almost silent rural valleys the industrial revolution changed all.

Iron was made first at nearby Llwydcoed and Abernant and then at Gadlys in what is now the centre of town. Pits extracting steam coal followed. A new canal was navigated taking expanding production seven miles down valley to join the existing Glamorgan Canal from Merthyr and run all the way to the port of Cardiff. Railways arrived in 1846. The 1801 local population of 1,486 increased exponentially to reach 54,000 in just over a hundred years. Outlying cottages became town houses. Terraces raced along valley sides, slung up by the owners of industry or their agents or some other Johnny come very recently here to make a swift buck from the working man's sweaty toil.

Places that were once entirely separate geographic entities merged. Fields were built on. Rocks were blasted, shaped, cut. On the map it's all Aberdare although locals won't praise you for suggesting that. They know, for certain, just where Trecynon finishes, with which street Gadlys starts, and where Foundry Town becomes something else. But mostly it's Aberdare, Aberdare the greater, rushed out to valley edge.

As a town this place does not like modern. Its public buildings, and it has quite a few, are mostly made of local Pennant stone and date from the mid-Victorian heart of industrial flourishing. Its chapels are more than many. They are great peak-roofed stone boxes which punctuate the lines of stone terraces in a flurry of Salem, Siloa, Bethania, Carmel, Siloh, Ebenezer and Bethel. Pubs, too, hang on here longer than elsewhere. They retail ale on most corners and next door to every church that Aberdare has.

John and I come up early from Queen Street. It takes an hour to wind between the ever-heightening valley sides. We stare out at the utter wrecked wood and broken brick decrepitude of the embankments and house backs. Has anyone cleared up here this century? Nope.

Aberdare once boasted three stations serving the Taff Vale Railway and the Great Western, and offered services on to Merthyr and to Abernant and through Hirwaun to the Vale of Neath. Service has now been reduced to a single track. This stops at a lamped iron buffer just north of the station's one platform. There are Welsh Government proposals that the line be reopened to Hirwaun with new station facilities but nothing yet. The new Aberdare campus of Coleg y Cymoedd opposite is on land that was once stuffed with engine sheds and coal sidings.

We cross south over the elaborate bridge spanning the bypass, test the facilities at the Sobell Leisure Centre (two disabled toilets and a machine dispensing bottled water by the door), before taking the underpass to hit the Cynon Trail north. Birdsong, leaf mould, rushing water. The sylvan valley as experienced by turn of the eighteenth century visitor B.H. Malkin returned in an exhilarating rush. The path we take was once also the route of the Llwydcoed Tramway. This was an early horse-drawn wagonway that brought the output of the ironworks at Abernant, Llwydcoed and at Hirwaun down to the Aberdare canal just to the west of us. Relics remain – embankments, a long line of limestone sleepers with plate holes still visible, a stream-crossing stone arch – but the glory is the cast iron Robertstown Bridge of 1811. It's still in place crossing the River Cynon at the eastern end of Meirion Street, Trecynon. This is one of the oldest surviving such bridges in the world. Its black cast iron arch looks like what it is – a new age interloper in the once pastoral calm.

From here the land rises steadily towards Aberdare Park. As local hills go this one is barely alpine although a few Cardiff flatlanders I know might have trouble with it. If I were Bill Bryson and John were his errant companion, Katz, slogging the Appalachian Trail, there would by now have been a run of disposed of items removed from John's bag and left in the bushes of local gardens in order to lose weight. But John is made of tougher stuff. He has brought with him hat, waterproof, dark glasses, shrink wrapped cake, bottled water, and two cameras, his regular Nikon D700 and, in addition, a Leica CL black and white film camera from the 1970s, carried in order to increase our project's range.

We divert along intersecting Mount Pleasant Street heading north to find Yr Hen Dy Cwrdd (The Old Meeting House), a Unitarian Chapel. The Unitarians were radical Christians who differed from most other sects by the refutation of the trinity and the rejection of the concept of original sin, predestination and the infallibility of the Bible. You'd think they'd be outcast but they flourished. Not conforming was (and is) a Welsh strength.

Unitarian spirit blazed right across radical Wales including here on the edges of the Aberdare industrial upheaval. The present chapel comes from the 1862 rebuild. In 1858, just before that monumental work, one of its congregation, Thomas Llewelyn, popularised publican James James of Pontypridd's tune 'Glan Rhondda' at the Llangollen Eisteddfod. The melody had a lyric to accompany it. "Mae Hen Wlad Fy Nhadau". This, of course, went on to become the National Anthem. In faded newsprint this story sits proudly in a battered glass case at Chapel front. But we can't get in. Hen Dy Cwrdd is barred and crumbling in the cold east wind. Chain and padlock on the gate. Wire fence to the side. Gravestones with their lettering flaking off. The spirit of this once powerful place appears completely drained.

A few hundred metres south stands The Coliseum Theatre. By contrast this is bright, repainted, and with lights on inside. Still alive despite the Covid knockback. It's a Cynon Valley enduring success. The Coliseum is an art deco theatre-cum-cinema, built for the use of miners in 1937 and, a few refurbishments on, remains an entertainment hotspot. John was here a year or so back to hear Andy Fairweather Low and the Low Riders replay the sixties as if they were yesterday.

Across the main Cemetery Road and through a tidy wrought iron gate lettered to celebrate the 1956 Eisteddfod Cenedlaethol is Aberdare Park. Grass cutters are whirring as we arrive, the flat green expanse revealed, a mild shock to eyes already becoming accustomed to bush and tree dotted hillsides. The Gorsedd Circle of standing stones could look Neolithically genuine if it were not for the clear sight of construction holes and the affixing of a prominent blue plaque. This commemorates David Williams – Alaw Goch – poet and pioneer of the coal industry and treasurer of the first National Eisteddfod of the modern era held in Aberdare in 1861. The great and the good hang on.

There are more historical celebrations at park exit. A stone likeness of Britannia, the robed and female god of industry, complete with anvil, cog wheel and hammer, stands in a state of contemplative ecstasy under the trees. She was presented to the people by the High Constable in 1905. Just what they wanted, no doubt. Nearer the gates Lord Merthyr, in the person of William Thomas Lewis turned into a bearded statue by Thomas Brock, stands on a plinth sat in decorative pool and surrounded by bedding plants. Lewis rose to fame and fortune as the

progenitor of Lewis Merthyr Consolidated Collieries. His million ton enterprise is presently the site of Rhondda's Heritage Park. The statue is in Aberdare because this is where the noble lord lived, at Maerdy House. To complete the valley breadth of this man's enterprise his body is buried in Merthyr.

After following Gadlys Road for a few hundred metres we turn into Elm Grove opposite the Mackworth Arms and the abutments that once carried a mineral railway. Beyond the redeveloped as flats Aberdare Girls School and in the garden of number 17 is a run of 1856 lime kilns. We are now in the centre of what was once the Gadlys Iron Works, a sprawling array of four furnaces, blast engines, coal stacks and casting sheds. Aberdare played a big part in the early iron trade sitting at the edge of that northern strip of ironstone land that ran from Dowlais to Ebbw Vale. The Gadlys furnaces were built into an embankment and sections are still visible further on where they today form part of the Cynon Valley Museum. Most, though, are lost to history under what is now Tesco's car park.

Turning back on ourselves along a short stretch of the A4233 we cross the green church yard of low rise and medieval St John's, an impressive remnant of an age that everyone else has forgotten. Nearby some of the town's few modern buildings cluster, the 1938 Council Offices, and the concrete slab and glass of the 1962 Central Library. With its café tables in the sun this pedestrianised square offers an unexpectedly cosmopolitan air. Centrepiece in a great circular plaque are the words of the poem 'The Mountain over Aberdare' recalling how it once was – "The drab streets strung across the cwm, Derelict workings, tips of slag." This is the work of Aberdare's most famous literary son – the Second World War poet Alun Lewis – who came from nearby Cwmaman.

Crossing what has to be the shortest and least impressive High Street in Wales the route reaches Canon Street near the 1831 original Town Hall. This is bustle land now. Shoppers, cars, the zip and zoom fate for the hearts of most conurbations.

Central Aberdare where Next and M&S do not jostle (but The Works, B&M, and Giovanni's Fish Bar do) is rich in Victoriana. Canon Street allows us to encounter, in quick succession, the ornate Constitutional Club, the enormous and crumbling 1867 Trinity Presbyterian Church, and then the vast 1500 seater 1858 Temperance Hall, now doing time as anonymously and plaqueless as it can as a beige painted branch of Family Shopper (Bargains everyday).

Not satisfied with its Queen of the Valleys appellation Aberdare, for a time, was also known as the Athens of Wales. Here at least three Welsh language newspapers flourished and countless books were published. Hard to credit now in a town where the language has retreated and the only book-shop, The Book Station, on Duke Street where the buses stop, sells second hand mass-market novels in cheap editions, stacked sideways on do-it-yourself shelves. When I asked in there for anything on local history I was told there was nothing today. But she'd keep an eye, if I'd like to call again.

Rhydwen Williams, novelist, crowned bard and editor of the influential Welsh medium cultural journal *Barn* made his home in Aberdare. When this titan of literature died in 1997 the *Aberdare Leader* got its linguistic knickers into a thorough twist and ran his photograph beneath the headline 'Great Loss To Literacy'. Says it all really.

Canon Street becomes Commercial Street and a right turn into the alley beside the Bush Inn allows access to Market Hall, appropriately on Market Street. This is the looming 1853 structure where local mine owner David Williams saved the day when the 6000-seater 1861 Eisteddfod Pavilion being erected on what is now Aberdare Park caught fire. The contest was held instead at Market Hall, the only place large enough locally. Chairs and stage equipment were carried across by Williams' workers. Holding the annual gathering in a building rather than a tent in a field is no new thing. John photographs an enticing run of bloomers, large tins, small cobs, large geese and milk loafs racked next to a sky high pile of corn beef pie slices offering enough calories to power a road gang. Beyond is a stall selling figurines from *Game of Thrones.*

Outside, Market Street loops back up Victoria Square, guarded at its eastern end by a miniature version of Lutyens' Whitehall Cenotaph. Next to the towering spire of St Elvan's Church[4] and attached to a great rock is a plaque which continues the National Anthem celebration seen earlier at Yr Hen Dy Cwrdd. This one celebrates the anthem's lyric composer, James James, who moved to Aberdare later in life and is buried in Aberdare Cemetery. His bardic name was Ieuan ap Iago. It follows you around, this magic song. John photographs. Next to Lulu's Hair & Beauty behind us stands the bard again, Yr Ieuan Ap Iago, a branch of Wetherspoons.

THE SOUTH WALES CHORAL UNION
COMPOSED OF 500 VOICES WON THE
CHIEF CHORAL PRIZE VALUED AT ONE
THOUSAND POUNDS IN OPEN COM-
PETITION AT THE CRYSTAL PALACE
LONDON IN JULY 1872 & 1873

Aberdare, Statue of Rhys Jones 'Caradoc'

Never wishing to allow history to dissolve into the dust as many places do Aberdare has another great celebrated with his arms waving at the top of the Square. Here, fronting the ancient (and now in considerable disarray) Black Lion Inn, is a statue of the great Victorian choir master Griffith Rhys Jones. Better known by his bardic name of Caradoc, Jones led the 460 voice Cor Mawr to win at the Crystal Palace contest of 1872/3. The world was conquered. When the train bringing the successful choristers home reached Mountain Ash cannon were fired. Drink was drunk. People clutched each other in glee. Goscombe John made his replica of the choir leader in 1920.

Day trippers might now wish to retreat to somewhere which offers the full Aberdare dining experience such as Servini's Café (est. 1933) on Cardiff Street. This enterprise appears large enough to seat coach parties and has a menu that runs around three walls. If the spirit is still with you, as it is today with John and me, a ramble up the steep valley side, actually Monk Street, is worth a go.

This steady climb passing at least three chapels along the way (including a very active looking branch of the omnipresent austere Unitarians) is the Maerdy Road into the Rhondda Fach on the other side of the Graig. It marks the edge of Foundry Town, a web of housing built to house workers when the nearby iron works was booming. Ahead is an example of colliery reclamation and land restitution rushed forward ahead of time following the Aberfan pit tip disaster of 1966. To sample this we turn right into Highland Place. This accesses the bed of the former Cwmaman Branch of the Great Western Railway which is now a path leading into the five-hundred acre Dare Valley County Park, land which was once occupied by at least four collieries. Views of the town below are splendid although nothing like those available if you were willing to slog the whole vertigo inducing zig zag right to the top.

But time is now not with us. We return to Monk Street walking below the water works. Evidence of iron castings hang on in the metal street name plates rusting into their housings and in a series of hefty iron gatepost finials in the form of black metal balls spiked above cast iron cushions which adorn the run of house entrances here. The finials are marked as Glancynon Foundry, W Williams Maker, Aberdare 1876.

We head into Foundry Town[5] down Ynysllwyd Street. The close and stepped terraced housing here is Victorian, stone built, squat and small. Constructed on a mix of Bute and Griffith Davies farmland the houses were built for local labour. If you had a Bute house (Bute Street, Dumfries Street, Nith Street) then you had slightly more room and a wider road than if you lived in a property constructed by Griffith Davies (Ynysllwyd Street, Catherine Street, Mary Street, Griffith Street).

After crossing Bute Street (this one resembling the more famous Cardiff version not at all) we reach the rail station out beyond the Newport-like Aberdare Bus Depot (café, toilets, shops, seats).

True valley adventurers such as John and I do not at this point give up and take the two-car south but head out west along Cwmbach Road to locate the head of the Aberdare Canal. Pieces remain but not much. Less than a kilometre gets us into the Canal Head Nature Reserve where a small section of the original basin and wharf complex remains full of water. Here plate ways and rail tracks met[6]. There were sheds and loading bays. Coal dumps. Cranes. Sidings. Today there is grass and there are bushes. Through the trees the original Canal Head House still stands and the rusted iron central pivot of a loading cane squats beside the duck-filled water. A zoom up a side path gets us a front view of the refurbished and with porch added blue painted structure. And then it's a stroll back to the rail station and more reflection on exactly why trains leave here mid-afternoon heading south and who it is that travels on them. Us, of course.

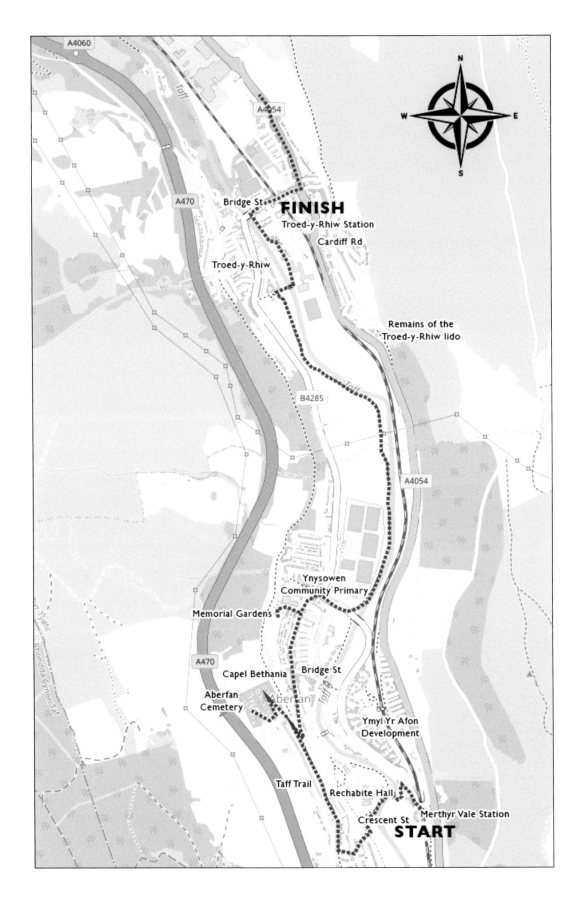

ABERFAN

4.32 miles
www.plotaroute.com/route/1718549
Merthyr Vale through Aberfan and on to Troed-y-Rhiw

North of Ponty the valley tightens and north of Edwardsville it tightens more. Cut by the combined Taffs, the Taff Fawr and the Taff Fechan from Cyfarthfa Castle and the Bargoed Taff at Quaker's Yard, it forms a steep-sided cwm so typical of how non-Valley residents think all these former industrial valleys are. To the west now lies Mountain Ash and beyond it, Aberdare. To the east, along the ridge edge of Cefn Merthyr runs a whole street of tumuli, barrows, cairns, standing stones and other pre-Roman relics. Despite industrialisation they are all still there. A vision of the valley past before we came.

We dismount the train at Merthyr Vale where the station with its narrow platforms and sloping access ramps from above resembles more a giant folding coat hanger than anything to do with rail.

Ynysowen, to give Merthyr Vale its older name, might well be where Owain Glyndwr fought the English in 1400. Before the industrial revolution the farm here had a field which was known as Owain's Water Meadow. Rumours of earlier revolutions persisted. It was in this place that bold John Nixon from Gateshead sunk his pit in 1869. Known first as the Taff Colliery it soon adopted the name of Nixon's Navigation Colliery, Merthyr Vale. Coal was extracted until as late as 1989.

Merthyr Vale Colliery Memorial

Merthyr Vale is now a memory of its former industrial self, in fact not even a memory. All that remains of the sprawling mine workings are half a pit wheel and a life-size wooden carving[7] of a miner holding a shovel. These are set in the centre of a roundabout. Out beyond them are the results of the council's great regeneration plan. The mine workings and tip remains have gone and in their stead are the new houses of the *Ymyl yr Afon* development. *Near the River.* Okay to build there now that river's propensity to flood has been contained.

This is an estate of detached and semi-detached houses built by Lovell Homes who market their new residences by giving each house style its own brand name. In the world of housing development these are usually things like *The Marlborough* and *The Dorchester* – names with middle-class resonance and considerable pretention. This time, however, the developer has chosen poets. They could have selected the names of well-known local bards – *The Idris Davies, The Sarnicol, The Leslie Norris, The Iolo Morganwg* – but they've gone instead for *The Keats, The Hardy, The Larkin* and then, amazingly, *The Abse.* Twenty-three examples of this one will be built. Dannie's house will have three beds, an open plan kitchen, and a valley outlook. He'd have been proud.

Nearer the rushing river a footbridge crosses to access the lower slopes of a rising stand of trees. The Council, Merthyr now we are within range, plans to put in more river crossings in order to bring the communities of Merthyr Vale and next door Aberfan closer together. Their Riverside Project will eventually result in two hundred and thirty new homes, a school, shops, restaurants and offices.

Rechabite Hall, four stories high, twentieth century construct, windows breeze-blocked and now clearly abandoned is pretty much all that remains of John Nixon's Nixonville. The hall and institute, begun as an outpost of teetotalism in 1914 and recently rebuilt as flats, stood at the head of Crescent Street with Taff Street beyond. Running close to the river both terraces were subject to constant flooding. They were demolished by the Council in 2018. Looking today it's hard to tell that the riverside here once teemed with working class life. Skirting Ysgol Rhyd y Grug, the path rises through the woods to cross the long abandoned line of the Quakers Yard & Merthyr Railway. We are now in Aberfan. A local walker tells me that the precise boundary between the two communities is the river and fixed forever no matter how many bridges the council build.

John who has his flat Dai cap on backwards making him look like an aged rapper has spotted the Halloween decorated local houses and is snapping them with his Nikon like fury. Ghouls, grim reapers and broom carrying witches peer from postered windows. Halloween charms and grave goods adorn walls. We're on the Taff Trail now, the hard metalled walking route that follows the line of the Glamorgan Canal along the side of the valley bound for Merthyr.

In their operational days the interface here between pit and canal had not been a happy one. The mining at Nixon's Navigation Colliery at Merthyr Vale had long resulted in local subsidence, notably below the canal itself. Sections in this area had reached twelve feet deep as the canal bed sank towards the pit workings four hundred feet beneath.

Ahead beyond the cleared site of the old Aberfan rail station is Aberfan cemetery. Its line of repeating white memorials once stood at the very top of the graveyard. Half a century of further burials means that they now run half way down.

On the surface there's little difference between Aberfan and any other valley former pit village. Closed chapels, boarded shops, houses for sale, pubs just about hanging on, people walking their dogs, a cheerful brickie building a garden wall. But below sits that past. The atmosphere a mix of memory, memorial, grief, and accountability. It all hangs on no matter what you do.

The disaster of 21 October, 1966 is one that if you were alive at the time you'll never forget. You will forever recall exactly where you were and what you were doing when you heard. It was an event like the Kennedy assassination or 9/11. Burned into consciousness. 144 dead, 116 of them children. A whole generation wiped out by the sliding of 40,000 cubic metres from number seven coal tip up on the mountain. The dust and coal waste originated at Merthyr Vale Colliery. It had been dumped on the mountainside on instruction from the National Coal Board. Underneath it was a mountain spring, which the NCB knew about but they dumped anyway. At 7.30 am the tip began to slide. No warning could be given by the men working on top. The cable from their phone line had been stolen and they couldn't have been quick enough to make any difference. The black came down the valley side in a wall storeys high.

The aftermath is well documented. The assistance, the sacrifice, the horror and the grief. A frantic digging by hand and shovel saved some but no survivors emerged after eleven o'clock. Faced with such overwhelming pain the community was rocked with a grief that lasted the rest of their lives. It's only now, perhaps, approaching sixty years on, that an easier world is emerging.

Up in the cemetery, which our walk passes, the burials run in two lines of pearl white granite. Quiet. Resonant. Names and dates. Few mentions of the actual cause of death. Passed away. Gathered in. Laid to rest. The names of all the dead repeated in a giant cross laid flat on the green hill. Visiting is an act of acknowledgement and of respect. Opinions differ as to who should be doing this. Dark tourism[8], a rising activity in west coast America, lists Aberfan as a place without what it calls 'commodification for tourism' and concludes that it does not want to be a destination. That's the sense we get too.

At the time ninety thousand donations amounting to more than a million and half pounds reached the Mayor of Merthyr's relief fund. If the disaster happened today that would be the equivalent of thirty-three million. Intended for the relief of those affected, given by a world population moved by the terrible news, the money proved difficult to spend. Procedural wrangling as to how and when and on what the relief resource should be spent continued for decades.

The Taff Trail runs on now, level, to the Memorial Gardens but we step off to walk down through Aberfan itself. No open cafés but hard to tell if this is as a result of the economy or Covid. John coughs, reminding me that he's just had it. The Aberfan Hotel still serving but closed when we pass. Capel Bethania, used as a mortuary during the tragedy, demolished and rebuilt in 1970 with fund finance in order to assuage the memory, is closed and has broken windows.

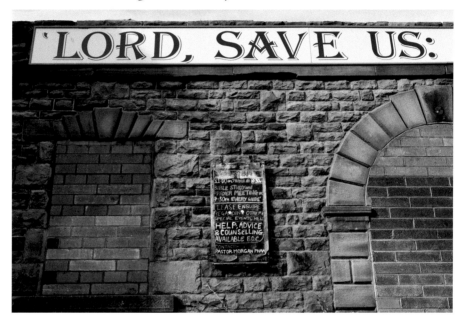

Aberfan Calvinistic Methodist chapel from 1876 complete with memorial organ furnished by the Queen was burned down in an arson attack in 2015. Its shell, emblazoned with the words 'Lord, Save Us: We Perish', still bears posters offering help to those in trouble. The three cinemas and run of shops selling everything from gents outfits to legs of lamb celebrated in local MP Huw Lewis' hugely readable memoir of an Aberfan nineteen sixties *To Hear The Skylark's Song*[8] are long gone. The three-storey Mackintosh Hotel, used by the Chief Constable as a reconnaissance point during relief operations standing at Aberfan's northern edge, is boarded and awaiting conversion to flats.

The memorial gardens, paid for by the fund, are as restrained and quiet as the line of grave markers. They occupy the precise site of the tip demolished Pantglas School. The similarly funded community centre and play area stand next door.

Across the valley the Coventry Playground is no more. It was built in 1972 on the site of the old Merthyr Vale School with donations from the people of Coventry and opened by their mayor. The land now houses an estate of eleven bungalows.

The replacement for Aberfan's Pantglas School, the new Ynysowen Community Primary, is down by the river, well away from the site of the disaster. Its spectacular timber-built structure comes complete with woodland walks, dipping pond, teaching glades and primary-age kitchen gardens. It was created by White Design Architects and resembles more a run of eco-age media offices than a school.

It could be that Aberfan has dealt with its past. Many of those involved have themselves passed on: the fund wranglers, the blundering politicians, Lord Robens, the National Coal Board chairman who refused to resign, who batted away blame and who demanded the disaster fund pay towards the tips' removal. The NCB itself. Even the good guys like First Minister Rhodri Morgan who in later years repaid[10] from Welsh Government sources interest on the monies which had been unconscionably taken. Not that fifty-five years alone can remove the memory.

This being a linear rather than a circular walk we take the riverside path north, horses in fields, soccer pitches, acres of woodland, the rushing Taff tumbling over weirs beside us. As valley towns go the gap between Aberfan and the next settlement north, Troed-y-Rhiw, is large. Green intervenes. Starts and finishes are unmistakable. But like everything else around here it isn't far.

This is Walter Haydn Davies country. Walter, the only poet as far as I can tell to have ever celebrated Troed-y-Rhiw and a writer with some rich pit tale-telling under his belt. Retired, slight of stature, face a run of Audenesque lines, long grey-brown coat always worn, Walter was a feature of south Wales literary gatherings up to his death in 1984. His set piece, brought out at any gathering where a floor spot could be found, was a ballad taken from his third book, *Blithe Ones*[11], which to the delight of audiences recounted a miner's trials searching south Wales for his lost wife. Everywhere from Cilfynydd to Coedpennau and Ynysybwl to Penrhiwceiber gets a mention and especially Troed-y-Rhiw. Walter came from Bedlinog just over the mountain and worked as a miner there. How pit life was in his century is beautifully recounted. I tell this to John as we near Troed-y-Rhiw's outskirts. He'd like me to sing it but I can't recall Walter's rumbustious tune.

Compared to somnambulant Aberfan, Troed-y-Rhiw is a vibrant place. Families on pavements. Delivery trucks. Purposeful walking everywhere. It's as if the slumbering valleys are readying themselves for bright Merthyr ahead. Troed-y-Rhiw, foot of the hill. The river crossing here is called PontRhun, Rhun's bridge. Rhun was Tydfil's brother, murdered here in the fifth century. A town history plaque suggests this might have been at the hands of pagans, "probably Irish". Local collieries were the Crawshay's Castle Pit (1866-1935) and the Plymouth Pit at South Duffryn (1862-1940).

Iron making happened just up valley. Never on the scale of the great ironworks at Cyfarthfa and Dowlais, Anthony Hill's Dyffryn Ironworks still had five blast furnaces working in 1870. Unlike many of his rivals Hill had a reputation for taking care of his workforce. He funded the building of St John's Church, a High Victorian Gothic construct on the west side of the river. He's interred there near the painted pipes of the large and ornate Gothic organ. He lies inside three coffins – oak, lead and finally elm, one inside of the other.

Along Bridge Street with the Angel Inn closed remaining pubs are returning to original form as drinking rooms opened inside terraced houses. They have scant signboarding but cheap ale. The Silver Bullet Free House offering wines, spirits and hot beverages is just along from the Belle Vue Hotel. In a window is a biro notice: 'Max capacity 50 persons'. Covid secure.

On the hillside, slightly off our route today but worth a visit for completists, are the remains of the Troed-y-Rhiw lido and changing rooms. That a town as small as this one should have possessed such a leisure facility amazed me. Financed by Llanishen publican Patrick Threipland and little bigger than a tennis court it was opened by Lady Stepney Howard in 1934. The period newspaper cutting I've seen shows Lady Howard making the opening speech in hat and floor-length coat. She is surrounded by Union Jacks. In the desolate 1930s the pool was much enjoyed. By the 1960s it has fallen from use and its remains today are an unedifying slop of weed and fractured concrete.

On the corner with Tyntaldwyn and Cardiff Roads where the world spins round are a pair of benches. Here you'd expect to find Walter Haydn Davies' retired miners, Shoni, Wil and Dai, passing the day sorting the problems of the world. But the benches are empty. Coal finished in the 80s. Retired miners don't last this long.

Out at the Merthyr end of town beyond the Eastern European £5 car wash on Holly Terrace are the town limits. Nearer at hand in café-free Troed is a tea machine at the Square Bakery opposite the bus stop. It took John and me, three shop assistants and ten minutes to get that device to work. The secret is to press the illuminated selection panel first. The bread pudding at £2.50 a fat slice is to be recommended. The rail station is back round the corner on Bridge Street.

Troed-y-Rhiw Lido

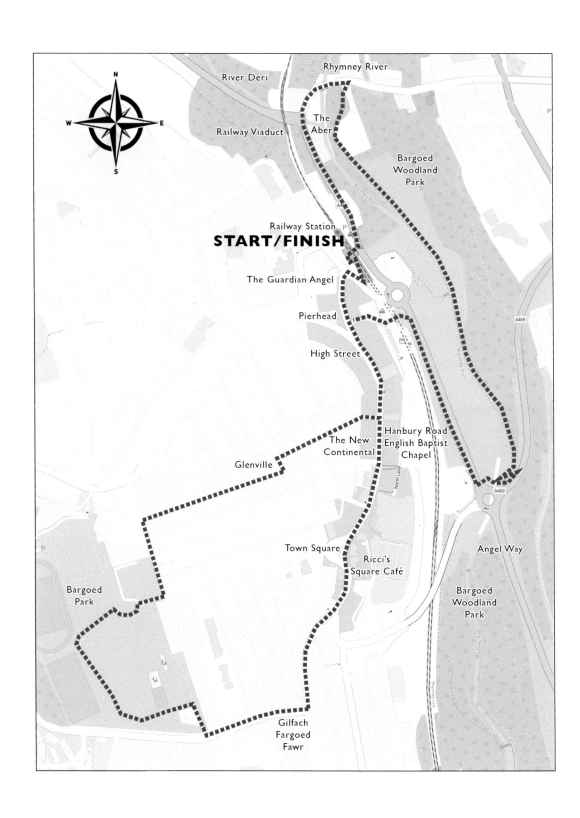

River Deri

Rhymney River

Railway Viaduct

The
Aber

Bargoed
Woodland
Park

Railway Station
START/FINISH

The Guardian Angel

Pierhead

High Street

Hanbury Road
English Baptist
Chapel

The New
Continental

Glenville

Town Square

Ricci's
Square Café

Angel Way

Bargoed
Park

Bargoed
Woodland
Park

Gilfach
Fargoed
Fawr

BARGOED

2.74 miles.
www.plotaroute.com/route/1038750

Bargoed feels different from many of the other Valley gateways, centres, towns and villages John and I have encountered in the creation of this book. This might be because, unlike the Rhondda or the Taff, its Rhymney Valley terraces are spread over a much gentler and somehow more agreeable set of slopes. The river that cut the valley has spread itself a little more. There's less drama and more light. Or maybe it's because Bargoed is a less overtly Welsh place than, say, Aberdare or Treherbert. But actually, I suggest, it's that its industrial past has by 2022 been totally and most successfully sanitised. Even the factory opened in the fifties for the employment of miners disabled by the dust to build peddle car versions of Austin cars for toddlers has closed.

EU money, when that was around, has poured through Bargoed removing the last traces of the giant pits that filled the valley bottom running across the map like black varicose veins about to burst. Bargoed was famous for having the largest coal tip in Western Europe, a colossal black sugar loaf towering over the trembling town. That has now been levelled. In its place are trees and grass.

Bargoed's main colliery, owned by Powell Duffryn, opened late, in 1897. By 1910 it employed nearly 2000 men and was the largest mine in the Rhymney Valley. It closed in 1977. As fans of industrial relics John and I try our best to locate what might remain. Tram tracks, rail line levels, chimneys, corrugated rooflines, metal detritus, coal darkness and dust. We find none. EU money has been pretty thorough.

Bargoed started life as a hamlet called Pont Aberbargod straddling both county and parish boundaries[12]. The rush for coal and the all-enveloping development of mass extraction pushed building south towards Pengam. The newly arrived Rhymney Railway built a station in 1858 and put up a nameboard with Bargoed on it and that was more or less that.

At its heart Bargoed had three pits: Britannia, Bargoed, and Gilfach. They are depicted through an industrial haze in L.S. Lowry's famous painting of Bargoed from 1965[13]. By contrast the works of painter D. Alun Evans in the nineties depict the tips removed and before regrowth has taken hold, the land in some sort of geometrically-driven agony, its crowning coal waste dispersed and its purpose totally gone.

We take a left out of the station to head down Station Road to view the triple wonders of the town. These are, taken in order: the great seven arch railway viaduct of 1858 which crosses Factory Road and is still in use carrying passenger traffic on and back from Rhymney; the contemporary bridge replacement for the original Pont Aberbargoed (actually not that much of a wonder in itself but embellished with a background of slowly curving terrace and period stonework it's worth a glance; and the actual aber, the confluence of the Rhymney with the minor River Deri or Darren (or to name it in more traditional and formal terms, the Nant Aberbargoed). This convergence of waters in February flood is quite something. Great gouts of white water bash at each other for superiority, the Rhymney winning as it rushes on ever south to Cardiff by the Severn Sea.

In the back garden of a house overlooking this mash of torrent the owner has created a display of flowering shrubs in pots and repurposed toilet bowls. They face down the rollicking river.

The once industrial black zone that was this place's raison d'etre is now Bargoed Woodland Park. It straddles both sides of the Angel Way, the bypass that has brought peace to the town's centre. The park, massive in both its purpose and extent has an ambience quite dissimilar to that of a regular municipal parkland. There's something different here mixed in with the bird warbling and the sound of wind through trees. Underlying it is the black dust just below (and often still on) the muddy and not yet entirely green surface. As a backdrop, too, there is the newly constrained and rechannelled Rhymney River thrashing like a beast through its gullies in a thundering, gulping gush. Few parks are ever this atmospheric.

Our path largely parallels the river (although diversions up slope into the reclaimed hinterlands are perfectly possible). High on the craggy bluff to our left are the backs of High Street and Hanbury Road premises. The Library declares itself with vertical lettering. A bunch of super giant daffs from public artist Malcolm Robertson colourfully mark the rear of the Bus Station car park.

Robertson, a successful Scot, was lead artist for Bargoed's four-year urban art renewal programme. He had a brief to work with local community groups and school children, the kiss of death for much art. However Robertson has triumphed, producing some of the best public pieces on view in the entire Valleys region. Entrepreneurs have been quick

River Rhymney and Woodland Park, Bargoed

to capitalise and a collage of Robertson's Bargoed art over-printed with the image of the War Memorial has been seen as an insulated mug, a phone case, and one-size fits all polyester leggings. Check Redbubble. Enterprise is everywhere.

We exit onto Angel Way next to Morrison's petrol station. The Woodland Park rolls on towards Pengam across land that once held some of Bargoed's eighty-six coke ovens as well as four irregular-looking square-sided and wood-slatted power station cooling towers. Before clearance they were photographed in their trackside location by Bernd and Hilla Becher. The Bechers spent fifty years photographing the emains of industry across the world. The result is an unrivalled archive of images of that industry reduced to its basic forms. Their black and white photographs are often made in large format and always present their subjects in the same front elevation. Flat, dramatic, unique, taken in hard and crisp focus with absolute precision. Their 1966 record of the Bargoed Cooling Towers is available as a print from J. Paul Getty for as little as £20.

Extending this Bargoed walk is certainly possible. The Country Park runs south into Pengam for a further mile and half of refurbished tip and vanquished devastation. Returning along the west of the river is one possibility as is catching the train back up from Pengam station via Gilfach Bargoed to Bargoed itself, the one we arrived at in the first place.

Our climb to the High Street takes us over not only the river but the rail line which, as part of the town's regeneration project (making Bargoed sound a little like Dr Who) has been covered to provide space for a new bus station. John shoots the landscape in the sun. Winter green. I try out poet Ian Duig's joke about the Catholic Priest, Church of England Vicar and Rabbit who go into a bar where the rabbit says, "I think I might be a typo" but John fails to laugh. Some jokes are better left on Twitter.

On High Street we both photograph Bargoed's most photographed building. This is the town's equivalent of New York's Flatiron, the Pierhead, otherwise the site of Bargoed's now closed department store, the Emporium. A sign outside announces that this significant commercial investment property will be offered soon for auction. It's dated April, 2016. To judge by the empty windows and rusted railings no significant investors have turned up yet.

Another Malcolm Robertson public artwork decorates the front. This consists of cut-out iron panels depicting the Emporium shop windows and is surmounted by a non-working cut-out of the Emporium's often non-working tower clock. Reality replaced with an image of reality, all colour gone.

We head left, up, along a street that, if not actually bustling, is at least alive. There are plenty of shops, a few more open than on an average day on Hannah Street in Porth, say, or on that dark stretch of Dunraven Street in Tonypandy. Barbers, hairdressers, Peacocks, the Rossi café, Modern Man Tattoo, Impressions Ladies Wear, the Just Because gift shop, the Square Royale café bar, then a run of shuttered fronts which either haven't yet opened (it's only 10.30 am) or maybe once did but now never will again.

In their centre stands the Hanbury Road English Baptist Chapel. This is an Edwardian Baroque styled, double-fronted masterpiece in red brick and grey Forest of Dean ashlar. The newly arriving English Baptists led by John Llewellyn built the place in 1906 and inside it's far more ornate than an austere Welsh-medium chapel might be. Fluting, arched friezes bearing Bible quotations[14], highly coloured engraved column finials, decorated trusses, embellished ceiling and an in place (although not functioning) organ which rises up behind the reception desk as if this were something out of 1984. The building has been refurbished (2011) and given new purpose as a town community centre and fully-functioning book-filled library.

Today there are more operational Italian cafés in Bargoed than might be expected, three at least in this town. Chain migration mainly from the Bardi area of Italy led to some 300 such Espresso-filled cafes being established in Wales. The Sidolis, Crescis, Contis, Cavallis, Antoniazzis, Fortes, Servinis and Strinatis were everywhere. The New Continental, a few paces on from the Hanbury Chapel, is one still in action run by the Strinatis and offers regular iced slices, carrot cake and cheeseburgers supplemented by a whole range of biscotti, all'olio di olivia, panini and other continental delicacies. The shop is immaculate, staff all wear uniform, and service is swift. The same family lived next door to me in Cardiff decades back. They were running Asteys then, another now lost Italian café, famous for its giant branch at Cardiff bus station. The Italian presence as restaurateurs, café owners and ice cream van operators throughout the south Wales Valleys has been well documented. But they are under threat. Times are hard. Do your best to help out. If you don't take a break here then Ricci's Square Café, a few hundred metres further awaits.

We are in Bargoed centre now. Town Square. Hanbury Square. Bargoed Square. It's called all of these things. Its dominant features are the fine-looking 1904 ionic columned miniature-monumental police court, designed by local architect George Kenshole and now used as a town hall, and the out of action Hanbury Arms with half its nameplate covered and a look of despair inside. Brightness comes in the shape of another Malcolm Robertson art intervention. This one, an absolute zinger, sits at Square centre. At first glance it gives the impression of Bargoed as somewhere in the high tide of the Soviet Union. Three 3.8m tall heads of miners emerge from the paving to dominate the whole vista. Their eyes may not follow you but their presence certainly does. For a moment I feel that I might be back in Budapest's Szoborpark, a parkland of retired giant Lenins and gargantuan out of favour Stalins. But these are the real people's heroes, pit heads, staring blindly out down valley onto the space where their places of work once were.

The walk bends on climbing slowly along Cardiff Road to reach a junction with Park Drive. Here stands Bargoed's oldest extant structure, the farm buildings of Gilfach Fargoed Fawr. This was once the operating hub of a nearly 300-acre farm with a recorded history going back to 1485. Most Valley towns are built on former farmland. It was the farm landlord's luck if he found minerals worth extracting underneath. Failing that he'd sell on as land for coal surface works or housing. Gilfach Fargoed Fawr farm owners, the Hanburys, managed both.

The allegedly haunted house that was left, with its rumoured but never located secret tunnel escape, became a doctor's surgery and then for years the RAFA Club. But even that today has fallen on hard times. When we get there the structure is barred and bolted, done in rain battered white-wash, high two storey with a low entrance door surmounted by a pointed Gothic arch that gives the empty place a medieval air.

The high climb up to Bargoed Skate Park pulls the legs but is again nothing like the standard in these climbs as set by Court Street in Blaen Clydach. If you are following these walks in the order they appear in this book then that is a joy that awaits you. Bargoed Park is high, neat, and municipal with no skateboarders visible and lacking totally sensations of the Woodland Park in valley bottom. We cross to exit through a maze of Victorian streets dotted with MOT garages, chapels, the Salvation Army and, on the corner of Upper Capel Street a terraced house bearing a rather small and somewhat battered plaque.

Glenville. This is the house in which the Anglo-Welsh war resister and poet who has haunted these narratives[15], John Tripp, was born in 1927, "and I want to know why[16]". The plaque was unveiled in 2015 in strong drizzle. A bunch of supporters including Robert Minhinnick, Sally Roberts Jones, Bob Walton, Clare Potter and myself read Tripp poems from beneath umbrellas and then the whole crowd of us retreated to the Capel Hotel in Gilfach for relief.

In its anonymity John and I almost miss the plaque and have to be directed back up Capel Street by a local. "These houses are full of history," she tells me. "That one," she points behind me, "used to be a shop." Where JT bought sweets, no doubt.

Capel Street rolls us directly back to town centre, passing Donna's Beauty Cwtch and the Retro Hair Studio, and into the arms again of the English Baptist's Hanbury Road Chapel masterpiece. We walk the length of High Street heading north. The shuttered fronts and empty windows of vanishing enterprise increase. Someone has tried hard with a contemporary knick knackery offering at least six plaques, paintings and signs composed from the word LOVE, one of them marked as 'Love, reduced now to £15' which is a price certainly worth paying. Next door a charity shop is offering a pair of not very distinguished second-hand trainers with the colouring flaking from the soles and wear marks around the lace eyelets as 'Alexander McQueen £50. Selling online for £350'. Bargoed is a fashion conscious place.

We pass the lost Emporium again and descend beside a gutted empty Woolworths to the street's finish by the Cosy Fish Bar. We are standing in a sort of square overlooked by St Gladys' famous Pritchard church with the town's war memorial rescued from vandalism and moved to the graveyard. In front of us Malcolm Robertson has sited another of his art interventions. This one is *The Guardian Angel*, a golden, slim and other-worldly figure on a four metre plinth pointing up to heaven.

If it hadn't been for the toast earlier John and I might well have diverted into Cosy's most appealing-looking fish bar. As it is we are both about as cold as we'd like to be and head downhill to the train station. The service is frequent, TfW units turning round here as well as those coming down valley from Rhymney. The one we catch will go on to Penarth, never a destination for black-faced miners but fair game for Bargoedians today.

Bargoed, if you don't know it, visit soon.

Malcom Robertson's *Guardian Angel*

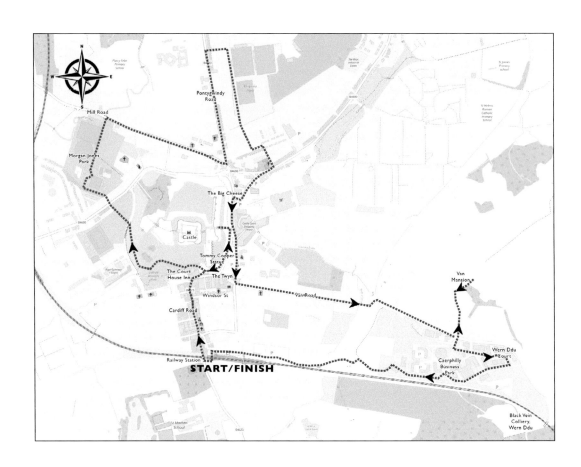

START/FINISH

CAERPHILLY

4.80 miles
www.plotaroute.com/route/916056

How far south do the Valleys run? As far as Taff's Well, as the locals there insist? Or do they stop at Pontypridd, which sounds sightly more realistic. Actually the real southern extremity lies elsewhere, I suggest, in spirit at least. Shrouded from the capital's urban razzamatazz by the bulk of its eponymous mountain Caerphilly has an atmosphere apart. Enough to make it a Valleys township? The jury is still out on that. By Valley standards Caerphilly is big and it has a huge era-defining castle right at its heart.

The town has also never been engulfed by the all-embracing proximity of large-scale coal extraction as have, without exception, all other Valley townships. Despite the presence of a Miner's Hospital and a Caerphilly Workmen's Hall and Institute (now reborn as a community arts centre featuring Mean Muscle Gym) Caerphilly seems unscathed by the remnants of large scale coal extraction that, with their tips and terraces and worn-out faces, are ubiquitous elsewhere.

Although Caerphilly was once home to a Roman fort it did not develop into a anything much until the Normans found themselves so threatened by the warring Llywelyn ap Gruffudd that they had to react. They began construction of what was to become the largest castle in Wales and, as it turns out, the second largest in the whole of Norman Britain. Only the one at Windsor is bigger. Stone built in a world largely made of wood Norman castles act as population magnets. In this one's wake was born the market town of Caerphilly – Kaerfily, Kerfyly, Cayfylly, Carfily or even Caerffili, the standard Welsh form of the name used today.

When coal began to loom in economic significance there were plenty of early attempts to work seams at the coalfield's southern extremity in Caerphilly. Old maps show innumerable drifts, levels and trial pits sunk into the mountain's northern escarpments. In the scale of things none of these ventures came to much. Visiting their sites today it's hard to discern that anything went on at all. Larger and deeper pits were sunk at Senghenydd, Llanbradach, and Bedwas, all several miles out from the castle and far enough away to allow their smoke and coal dust to settle elsewhere.

Not that this stopped Caerphilly from becoming an

industrial success. Coal shipped through here. The railways dominated along with the ancillary trades that railways bring. The Rhymney Valley Railway established their works south east of the castle and built and repaired a whole railroad's worth of engines, brake vans, carriages and wagons. A massive tunnel was drilled through the mountain to the port at Cardiff to enable the coal to reach its larger market. The town had a heyday. And a half.

Today Caerphilly is largely a dormitory for Cardiff and, with that unmissable castle, a tourist destination. It has an aerospace sector and logistics operations run from the local industrial parks built on the swathes of land subsequently vacated by obsolete coal sidings and outmoded engine works. It has social housing in vast estates and a shopping centre with aspirations. It might well have overcome the purpose-lessness of some of the towns higher up the valleys but, despite its assets, in Caerphilly the air is not yet of sophistication or urban bustle. It is as if Caerphilly is still thinking about what to do next.

John and I have caught a fast two-car train up so quick that by the time we've got on it's time to get off. The four minute-long black rattle through the nearly two kilometre tunnel still provides a thrill. I read some-where that this tunnel will not be electrified and that future transit on the South Wales Metro will be by battery. Not really very reassuring but other than hopeful slogans[17] along the sides of diesel units the arrival of change is slow.

Caerphilly Town Centre

Caerphilly station serving a town of around 35,000 ought to be grand but, compared to the still-extant Victorian magnificence of Pontypridd, it's nothing much. A couple of platforms and a siding, two footbridges and an operating kiosk. Although as the station is a potential tourist gateway to the town and the Metro is coming there are plans afoot for a comprehensive redevelopment. But at the time of our visit that's still to happen. I buy a banana and John gets a bottle of water.

We take the easy slope down Cardiff Road towards the Castle. This is Caerphilly shopping central with more stores unboarded and open than is the case in most of the Valleys. Towards the bottom, beyond the ancient-looking Kings Arms, Stockland Street and Windsor Street have both been blocked to traffic creating what, back in the new millennium, the planners referred to as "intimate public squares populated by sculpture". The sculpture turns out to be a series of pillar-mounted metal birds created by Julie Westerman. At Stockland Street these are jackdaws, at Windsor Street they are geese. "They're new, they are," a bench-sitting pensioner tells me, "the ones they had before have been nicked".

As Cardiff Road flattens out there's another ancient tavern, The Court House Inn. This one trades out of what was originally a medieval court house serving the Lord of Glamorgan. Beyond it, the Ddraig Goch flying from one of its towers, the castle floats like a million-pound extra from *Lord of the Rings*. Tourists perambulate its circumference, the medieval fashionable again.

Fronting the castle is more public art. This time an internally illuminated, unlabelled twelve metre slim and pointed obelisk created (I find out later) by landscape architects Camlin Lonsdale and looking like a south Wales model of the Shard but lacking that edifice's purpose. What's it here for? Who knows.

The Twyn, the town's central square, is home to a very contemporary-looking and pretty enormous tourist information centre. Not that there's much actual tourist information available inside. One rack of leaflets, a pile of pocket-size Caerphilly cheeses (made in Cenarth, west Wales), and a café. Next door Caerphilly's claim to world-wide fame as the birthplace of Britain's leading error-prone conjuror, Tommy Cooper, is splendidly celebrated.

Cooper was a marmite man. Either he made you fall about laughing just by walking on stage, or you hated his whole anti-intellectual stance. He died mid-performance on live TV in 1984. Since then his reputation has steadily risen.

His act ages well. He was born a mile away in Llwyn On Street although he barely stayed there three years before his parents moved to Devon. Local pride and pressure from the Tommy Cooper Society resulted in a nine foot bronze statue of the fez-wearing magician[18] being unveiled in the heart of the town. Behind is a slightly bent bi-lingual sign advertising the Tommy Cooper Walk of Fame. With unintended civic irony this turns out to be a sloping stubby and joke-free stroll on tarmac along the Castle's front. Local supporters have had their names engraved on bricks set below a bunch of benches. The biggest is the one paid for by Society patron Sir Anthony Hopkins.

Castle Street naturally leads on to Caerphilly Castle itself. This is the Marcher Lord Gilbert de Clare and cohort's monster defence against all comers and specifically local all comers. He built it in 1268. Today, at £7 a day trip, it's a bargain. Cadw, who manage the upkeep, have clearly been selling themselves short. But then this is not £35 Madam Tussauds in central Marylebone but a pile of stones in rainy De Cymru. For your money you get to see close up a multi-ring circus of medieval towers, redoubts, dragon pits, defended islands, defensive moats, wooden siege engines, great bastions, arrow slits, towers and battlements that make up the most dramatic preserved castle I've ever encountered. In addition to Norman swordsmen and Welsh serfs, the Zutons, the Stranglers and Ocean Colour Scene have all also played here. It's possible, if your predilections run that way, to hire the place for weddings. Ever since the then owner, the third Marquess of Bute, reroofed the great hall in 1871 for a great meeting of the Royal Archaeological Institute, the Castle has been a venue that's hard to beat.

But if you don't have the time and today we don't then even a traverse of the perimeter is inspiring. The great leaning south east tower, 10 degrees out of perpendicular, appears to defy gravity. It was not blasted by Owain Glyndwr in his rebellion of 1403 which many of us would love to believe but was deliberately blown up in 1642 during the Civil War. From then until the first Marquess of Bute acquired the castle by marriage in 1776 the structure languished.

The Butes, great landowners, Scottish financial overlords of much of south Wales' wealth, had a history of restoration and did much to record, preserve, and rebuild the castle. The fourth Marquess, John Crichton Stuart, took a special interest. That's him in twenty-foot wooden effigy[19] standing below the leaning wall with his arms holding it up.

Currently CADW are investing heavily in the castle's future. A new visitor centre, toilets, a massively revamped medieval Great Hall, new interpretation throughout and all preceded by thorough and deep archaeological research. The Welsh media are suggesting that this five million pound investment will attract more tourists. It certainly better.

The route runs on through parkland beside the castle's lake. There are geese and duck everywhere, bold ones, standing on the paths demanding to be fed, others squawking in the air. The exit is across Nantgarw Road to a further Caerphilly green space, Morgan Jones Park. This large, multi-use

municipal space (bowling green, kids splash pad, skateboard ramps, outdoor gym, grass maze, the complete public outdoor space works) celebrates the famous local World War I conscientious objector and MP for Caerphilly. There's a plaque if you look hard enough. Morgan Jones, 1885-1939, former Council chairman, Caerphilly MP and Baptist lay preacher. Qualities you don't see a lot of these days.

Mill Road, named for the Energlyn corn mill which once stood in Morgan Jones' north-western corner and of which there is now naturally not a sign, once led to the gas works and the Double Diamond Club. Named after a famous bottled beer this workingmen's club rose to south east Wales fame in the 70s when it outdid anything Cardiff had for drink and entertainment. Unbelievably the Big O played here, as did Johnny Cash, both fighting the career downturns that the music biz often brings. Roy Orbison sang every night for a whole week in the 1970s. By the eighties, though, after joining Bob Dylan in the Travelling Wilburys, his fame returned and Caerphilly ceased to be the fee-paying draw it once was.

We head east for Pontygwindy Road to see what remains of Caerphilly's Co-operative Garden Village[20]. Rhiwbina in Cardiff was not the only place in south Wales where co-operative working class housing flourished. There are a number of garden villages here in the Valleys. Not that that word is quite the right one for what happened here. The idea was good, one hundred well-designed be-bathroomed houses planned and land bought. But only eight actually built. Financial difficulties and loss of will got in the way resulting in the land being sold off and the greater plan abandoned. The houses actually erected (no's 69 to 83) are currently not in the best of repair. They are in a run fronting the main road. A large service station called Caerphilly Garden Village Garage sits next door.

The owner, standing next to life-sized statues of a golfer in mid swing, an Alsatian dog and a quarter-size hippo, is wearing a Boston Red Sox hat. John engages him in conversation and discovers that he's just come back from tourist capital Sarasota in Florida. John, a northern Minnesotan, has never been there. But he has managed Pigeon Forge, the world's tackiest inland resort, stuffed-solid with the sort of games machine, cheapo drink and outré entertainments that would make Magaluf appear the height of sophistication. So, too, it seems, has the owner. The two share notes.

Disappointed with the Garden Village but at least pleased we've located it we head back into town. Some things in life are never funny – battles, Castles, flowering plants, embroidery. But others always are – fish, porcupines, and top of the list, cheese. Although maybe not Caerphilly's example, celebrated here with the Big Cheese statue. This looks like a spray-concreted mini-roundabout with a slice missing and sits at the junction of Bedwas Road and Castle Street.

Caerphilly cheese has not been made in Caerphilly in an age. Best current source is the one the Tourist Information Centre uses, Caws Cenarth in Boncath, Carmarthenshire. Originally the cheese tasted very different from the current rather pasteurised product. Caerphilly ended up as the generic term for cheese made out the back by most south Wales farmers. It was softer than cheddar and often consumed by miners who found it a ready portable snack. It was sold at Caerphilly market. The name attached by osmosis.

During World War II the Ministry of Agriculture diverted what milk the country had to Devon for the dairy industry there. Local production of Caerphilly Cheese ceased never to really recommence, although there have been attempts. In the battle for the universal cheese Cheddar wins, it seems. Looking at the white surface of the cheese statue slowly grubbing black in the traffic that might be just as well.

We walk east along the length of Van Road. Van from the Welsh Y Fan meaning either damp ground or hill. Those seeking freedom from accompanying traffic might well want to divert onto the parallel and much quieter Maes Gwyn but we tough it out. Beyond the Van roundabout and after the road crosses the most appropriately named Scouring Brook the yards of plant hire and caravan repair operators signal the arrival of Caerphilly Business Park.

With 158 companies registered this enterprise is of considerable size and, to judge by the great inland sea of vehicles flooding its car parks, a considerable success. It was originally known as the Harold Wilson Industrial Estate. But despite for a short time looking as if he might put the world's ills to the sword that pipe-smoking giant of British Labour politics has fallen from favour. But, first, Van Mansion itself.

This is up a farm lane from the short run of nineteenth century houses built for Rhymney Railway workers. The privately-owned Van Mansion, or Castle as its hopeful interpretation sign declares, is a fine example of Elizabethan manor building. A mile across the valley from the real castle it was put up in its present form by Thomas Lewis in 1583. It was the grandest habitable house in these parts for centuries. Lewis got permission from the Earl of Pembroke to use stone liberated from the by then crumbling Norman Castle to enhance his distinctive yellow sandstone four gabled profile. You can spend hours here spotting the whiter former-Castle stone from the newer dressed material that Lewis had to quarry elsewhere.

For much of latter part of the twentieth century with a failed roof, listed status and outrageous refurbishment costs it looked as if the Van would go the way of many of Wales' lost mansions. But a change of ownership and a campaign of support brought the place back from the brink. Repairs are still ongoing. Builders' vans dot the grounds. A sign on the gatepost also warns that this is private property. That sentence is underlined. It suggests visitors navigate their way on to nearby Llancaiach Fawr[21] if they are searching for the full Elizabethan historical experience.

Round the back, viewable (just) from the public road is a huge thousand-berth pigeon shed or columbarium, also listed[22]. This fell down in the deep freeze winter of 1947 but has now been superbly restored and, if it were situated on the Cardiff foreshore, could be mistaken for part of a Victorian sewage works or a giant World War II gun housing.

Looking back downhill to the Business Park, everything is tranquil. Among the greenery of the lower mountain once stood Black Vein Colliery, Wern Ddu, the nearest actual pit to Caerphilly itself. Not a trace remains. Not much, if anything, either of the great Rhymney Railway works that stood here clanking and steaming, 1901 to 1964, building, repairing and testing the motive power and carriage stock of an entire railway system. The sheds, as they were locally known, became the Western Region's largest outside Swindon. Their ghost echoes as the hooter from a southbound TfW four car rushes to Cardiff along the track behind its screen of trees.

The Business Park offers considerably more than the logistics, alarm companies and office furniture suppliers that I'd at first expected. In addition there are as many public and white-collar operations here as there are light industrial.

Creditsafe, Domus Ventilation, Disability Wales, Acorn Recruitment, Inprova Energy, Blue Butterfly Weddings and the South Wales Spine Centre all operate out of recent-build pink and orange brick.

We track across looking for engine works, railway remnants, sleepers, and dirt, but there are none. Even the Caerphilly Railway Society which had a few engines here at the end of the twentieth century has been ousted by Caer Workplace Health Specialists and the purple-doored premises of Brumble Security. At the eastern extremity, though, stand the Victorian red brick gable ends of what was originally part of the Rhymney Railway's engine repair operation. These sheds operate out of what is known today as Wern Ddu Court and now house the works of JJ Castings Ltd.

These premises are not open to the public but a smile from me and a Minnesota-accented "Good morning," from John get us through the door. Our tour is led by live-wire company owner Theresa Rees. Inside the sheds there's a palpable railway atmosphere despite no engines having been repaired here since the steam tanker 5203 was fixed sixty years ago. Traces of smithy chimney snake up the unadorned red brick sides. There's a still operating 10-ton Cowans Sheldon transverser crane from the Victorian dawn of railways and the remains of hoists and lifts. Metal-hardening furnaces stand where the axel-box shop and wheel roads once did.

The original sheds had a high slate roof and ventilation windows. These have gone but the rest still looks like it did when first built a hundred and twenty years back, a house for fire and smoke. When the last steam engine[23] left the works in June, 1963 it did so as a fire-breathing dragon. Workers had riddled the tracks in with fog detonators right up as far as the main line station. The resultant explosions to the accompaniment of wild cheering and the blowing of whistles made it seem as if the end of the steam era and the work that went with it was a thing to celebrate.

After tea and a kit-kat and a few shots taken of Theresa operating one of the frighteningly hot furnaces we return to our route. Visitors following us should view this unexpected remnant of south Wales former transport mainstay from the car park. Unless, of course, they have some castings that need thermal stress relieving in their rucks.

The path exits the western end of this enterprise zone to follow the edge of the rail line towards Caerphilly station. This takes us through both the significantly full park and ride, solid proofs of town's present-day Cardiff dormitory status, and the bus station.

Caerphilly's railway era gets a final hurrah in the host of black and white steam train photos decorating the inside walls of the ticket office. As far in the past as Napoleon or the Egyptians to most present-day travellers. The train back is empty but that's never the case at rush hour. Route followers take note

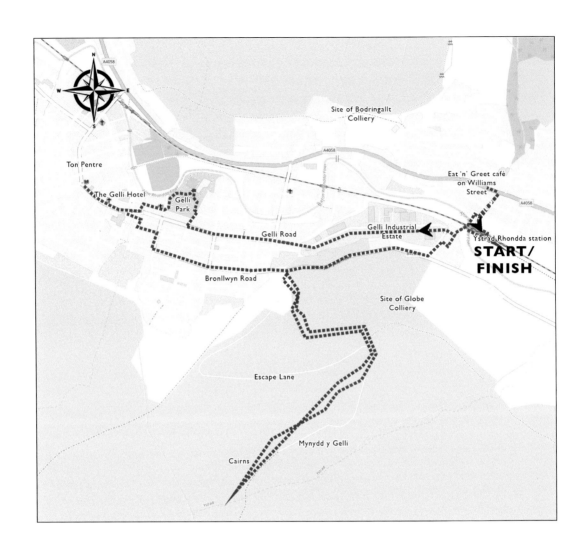

GELLI

4.33 miles
www.plotaroute.com/route/955821

In the ribbon run of valley villages knotted around the sites of their pits Gelli should be no different from any other. Strings of worn out pubs, cafés, deserted Miners' Institute in Victorian red brick, statue of a worthy, a plaque or two, sites of the pit heads memorialised with a black coal-filled dram. The past still present. But not here.

Even the Gelli terraces filling the omnipresent valley sides here refuse to look wan and battered by time. Their blocks are repointed, their windows replaced, their front doors Dunraven glorious and their small front gardens, where they have them, lawned evergreen with green grocers' artificial grass.

The attraction to us of this place is not its history of pit, coal dust and unending toil – although those have been significant enough – but rather its mystic mountain. It's there, high up above us in its megalithic fern-overgrown fuzziness, rays of Blakean sunlight breaking across its Iolo Morgannwg stones. This Gelli episode will reward the determined walker with numinous wonder – if their luck and belief sustains them and the rain gods hold back – but only after a certain amount of perseverance, and naturally having first traversed the town.

We reach this Rhondda outpost, as ever, by rattling train. It departed from Cardiff late and spent its long rolling sway of a journey trying furiously to catch up. The further north we travel the tighter the valley sides get. Views close in. Mostly green now in place of dust and coal tip black.

We get off at Ystrad Rhondda station. This is the nearest for Gelli and brand new in 1986 although maybe looking slightly run down now. Pale sunlight reaches in through the morning's gloom. In the distance we can hear birds and the sound of the river tumbling. Do we head off immediately? No. We hunt out the nearest place for tea.

This turns out to be the Eat 'n' Greet café on Williams Street. On the wall is a cluster of photos, nine of them, headed 'Wall of Shame' next to a second board headed 'Wall of Fame' and containing only one. This is the café's Big Breakfast Challenge where an impossibly huge array of sausages, fried eggs, toast, bacon slices, black pudding and the rest are on offer for free if you can get them all down in less than 40 minutes. £15 if you can't. We pass.

Gelli, Rhondda Fawr River bridge

The mystery of just where Ystrad ends and Gelli begins is solved by the café owner who tells us it's over the bridge. The one in question is box girder and spans not only the loop of tracks that is the Gelli main line but that rushing river. This surprisingly vigorous waterway had, until comparatively recently and like many valley rivers, a long history of over-flowing its banks and filling the dry local houses with wet muck. As if the dry muck they habitually got was not enough. The solution was the Rhondda Wall, a line of steel sheet piling of significant depth banged into the river edge by constructors using heavy equipment not seen in these parts since the pits were sunk. The result is a river-repelling dry fix. Everyone is happy, for now.

We cross up and into the Gelli Industrial Estate strung out across land once occupied by Gelli's justification, the Globe Colliery. This was originally sunk into the Royal Navy-approved bituminous coal seams by George Griffiths and Edmund Thomas in 1870, bought out and much deepened by John and Richard Cory in 1894 and managed by them until nationalisation in 1947. At its height the pit employed over 900 men. It closed in 1962.

The Estate offers the expected mix of small semi-industrial operations, those capable of hanging on by dint of actually reaching a profitable market. UPVC windows, car tyres, food distribution, road surfacing, a gym, and a Christian charity mixing God with sport for the schools of the Rhondda. There's no sign I can see of the pit head or the baths or the coke ovens or anything at all that says this was once the great enterprise it reputedly was. At its end the town begins, terraces in a grid above the twisting river.

On Gelli Road, the main drag, we pass houses, two up two down, with hearts hanging on raffia in their front room windows. The tight brick premises of the Gelli & Ton Hibernia Workingmen's Club & Institute offer shots at a pound a go every Saturday. Centrepiece, if such a designation holds, is the bold and very contemporary-looking Crispy Cod. Finest fish and chips since 2008. It's done in tasteful grey, wood clad, and looking more Ikea than Valley legend.

Turning right, back towards the river, is Gelli Park. This is a brief oasis of traffic-free grass, locked bandstand, bowling green and winding walks. It opened opposite the Ystrad sawmill in 1919 and a hundred years later is still breathing. We are the only visitors. The exit opposite the Hope Baptist Church leads us on to the end of town.

Bethany Methodist Chapel from 1886 still stands, crumbling. Rebuilt in 1929 this simple gothic structure hung on long enough to get planning permission for demolition and replacement with flats in 2007. In the capital they would have a built high-rise student accommodation on the site in double quick yet here, where the world's demands are much simpler, it's a decade on and still nothing has happened. Ahead of us, as Gelli Road bends imperceptibly north, Ton Pentre begins.

On the border stands The Gelli Hotel, bristling with flower baskets and satellite dishes. It has been brashly repointed and rewindowed and is clean enough to shine in the sunlight. Perfection. Except that the letters of its name plate, the THE and the GE have all been stolen. Only the LLI remains. This place, in its smoky past, was where the first Miners Federation of Great Britain lodge was formed at the end of the nineteenth century.

To the south, on hillside now once again greening, David Davies Llandinam[24] sank his Eastern Colliery, Gelli's second pit, in 1877. It operated until 1937. We walk back the few hundred metres to the Crispy Cod and then turn up Tudor Road to sample the entirely similar terraces of Stanley Road, Alexander Road and then Bronllwyn. Bronllwyn Road was where my grandfather lived with his young family, back when it was brand new in 1911. Rented, naturally. Nobody owned property then.

I knock on the door which is answered by neat and blue cardiganed Ann Jones. She has lived here for 77 years, she tells me, amazed that a memory from before her time should come enquiring. My grandfather, a signalman, lived here and then left well before she was born. He worked for the Taff Vale Railway. Her grandfather who built the house did too. So that was the connection – trains. We smile and John photographs us. The day rolls on.

On the other side of the valley are the still just about visible tips and mounds from Bodringallt Colliery. Lines of black coal waste discernible among the encroaching trees. High above on the skyline is a line of wind turbines. The new pylons, ever-present, marching across the landscape. They jar my vision today but as time makes them ever familiar soon they won't.

The town runs back out almost as quickly as it arrived. Bronllwyn Road tips us onto the faster Nant y Gwyddon, site of the Globe Colliery below us, Mynydd y Gelli above. As mountains go this one is no giant but it still goes up. Climbing it should take a mere 30 minutes, tops.

Finding the path is not easy. Along the main road is the entrance to find the entrance to the former Nantygwyddon Landfill Site is now gated and closed[25]. All references to its previous life as a civic amenity are mossing slimy green in the damp autumn air. The bold will simply ignore the official notices banning it and squeeze themselves easily through the chain fence and take the well surfaced zigzag road to the top. This is marked as Escape Lane on most maps and was the route formerly used by lines of refuse trucks climbing the heights to rid the Rhondda of its household waste. The enterprise at the summit has now been capped but as methane still escapes it's officially out of bounds.

If you do take the route up Escape Lane then a stile accessing the formal waymarked mountain top path appears on your right towards the top. Non-trespassers like us will take the advice of the white van man standing smoking nearby. "Go left there by that hut over by there," he tells me, pointing. "Lots of people go that way. But it's a climb, mind, a climb". Hell, it is.

The path, unwaymarked but pretty obvious for most of its ascent, is largely up and up and then up again although it does have a few forays on the level from which you can observe Gelli, Ystrad and Ton Pentre spread below in all their terraced glories. Realisation dawns slowly although it shouldn't have taken me so long. What we are climbing up is not a grass-covered gentle mountain at all but a successfully reclaimed coal tip. Pieces of anthracite protrude from the path. The run-off is black. The whole surface has the sagging moon-soft feel of stuck together dampened dust.

On the OS two dotted parallel lines to the top mark not a Roman road but the line of the one-time pit coal waste cable cars. Their poles and their wire ways are now gone for scrap. All that remains is a residue of the stuff they once carried.

Top of the mountain are more gates along with an extended run of chain fencing which protects the tip gas escape management centre. Lads on bikes would rip the surfaces up here if they could gain access. There are signs around us banning them. Kawasakis and their black helmeted riders like dark-hatted cowboys in the American west. We take the stile on the right to access the grass and fern humped plateau which now spreads off for many miles in all directions. Head south and you'll reach novelist Lewis Jones' former house in Clydach Vale or go further and it'll be poet Sam Adams' place in Gilfach Goch.

But our destination is much nearer to hand. This part of the mountain flat top holds what some over-zealous modern antiquarians and megalithic portal followers have dubbed the Welsh Stonehenge. Well, it's not quite that. Nothing like that at all in fact. But up here among the collapsed farmers' walls and the glacial erratics are cairns, standing stones, house plat-forms, ancient field systems and a half extant stone circle. Are these the remains of another saucer landing site, a megalithic star observatory, a stone-era masonic temple, or a holy site of human sacrifice? Today it is none of these things. Under the slate grey and threatening drizzle and overgrown by a whole summer's mountain fern the tenacious stones in their ancient formations simply glower.

A pattern appears, through the centuries, among the ways we treat these venerable objects. In some eras they mean nothing and are ignored. In others their pagan presence is an insult to the prevalent religion and they need to be removed. Often their stones are stolen for re-use elsewhere. Farmers recycle them as gateposts or smash them to provide building materials for barns and houses. Across south Wales there are many examples of fractured memorials, debonded cromlechs and earthen barrows ploughed flat because they were in the wrong place and acted as a barrier to the movement of cattle.

On the Wiltshire plains a great stone circle has completely disappeared. The Sanctuary was a set of concentric circles of standing stones on Overton Hill overlooking West Kennet long barrow. It was recorded standing by the antiquarian John Aubrey in 1649 who brought the king to see them and then again by William Stukeley in 1723. Both men made drawings. But the landowner, farmer Green, felt they stood in the way of his agricultural ambitions and were a pagan slight to the power of Christianity. Sometime in the mid eighteenth century he began their removal by smashing them to manageable pieces and carting them off. By the time he finished all that was left were the post holes. The poet Adam Thorpe describes this vandalism with fury in *On Silbury Hill*[26], his beautifully written ride through the remains of British Neolithic power. in the mid-nineteenth century the lost stone locations were marked by the insertion of concrete posts. The shape preserved but the atmosphere damaged. Better than nothing, but only just.

It could be that a farmer Green has been in action here amid the once powerful circles. The government's Coflein web site[27] offers the precise co-ordinates of the Mynydd-y-Gelli remains but among the overgrown tumbles that run before me these hardly help. We stand and stare on at the tree and grass strewn horizon. I try for that sense of power and wonder that often fills high places. The uplift, the thrill, the suprahuman silence. Nothing. I'm clearly here on the wrong day.

The route back down we take is a stroll. Zigzag zigzag and then back out through that chain link gap. Should we be going this unofficial way? Officially we should not.

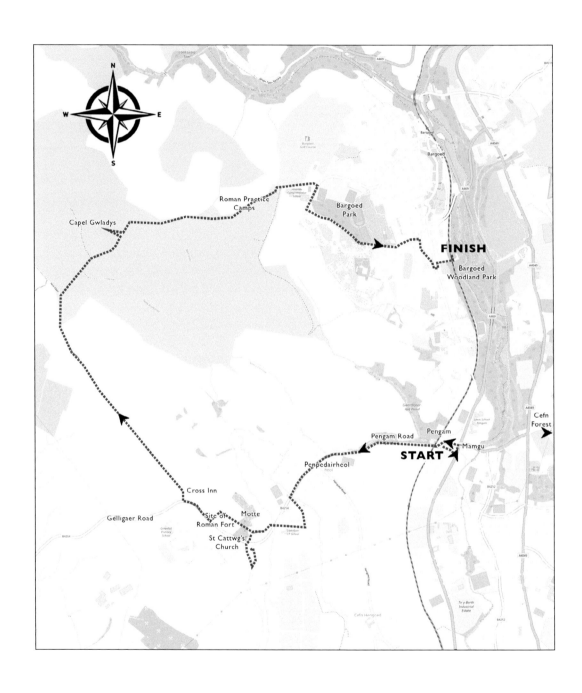

N
W   E
S

Roman Practice
Camps

Capel Gwladys

Bargoed
Park

FINISH

Bargoed
Woodland Park

Cefn
Forest

Pengam Road   Pengam

Mamgu

START

Penpedairheol

Cross Inn

Gelligaer Road

Site of
Roman Fort

Motte

St Cattwg's
Church

GELLIGAER

6.45 miles.
www.plotaroute.com/route/1658108

All the forecast apps on my phone show dry today. Gentle breeze, zero precipitation. No chance anywhere of rain. But out of the window it's still drizzling. Valley weather. We're at Pengam on the Rhymney Valley line, one hundred and seventy car park spaces (mostly vacant), ticket machines and a locked toilet. By way of conversation the station guard tells me that the recent long run of summer weather has played havoc with his racing pigeons' homing abilities. He's right. I look around and can't see a one.

The station where we've alighted is on the west side of the Rhymney River in a place known today as Glan-y-Nant. On the river's eastern bank is Pengam proper where the town's second station on the now uplifted Brecon and Merthyr Railway was once situated. Britannia Colliery sprawled between the two.

We walk downhill passing a small cluster of shops which includes two bakers and a motorcycle spares store to inspect the small park on the corner of Cardiff Road and its contentious 'landmark' statue. The park, built over a culverted tributary of the Rhymney, Nant-y-Cascade, is embellished with a thirteen metre tall steel and resin block sculpture created by Portsmouth artist Pete Codling. This is of a mother-figure emerging from the ground and gazing in supplication to the past or the future, or possibly both, in the direction of Bargoed. The artist calls it *Mamgu* although residents have other names. The media have dubbed it *The Lady of the Stream*. Giacometti it isn't. Controversy has dogged it with locals claiming that not only does it not look safe but it reminds them of an erect penis. "It's only when you come from Bargoed you can see the face of the woman" claimed one.

Ahead through the depths of Pengam and up the rising eastern valley side lies Blackwood. Somewhere in between and built at a time when there was nothing else at all in between bar woodland and farm track lies Cefn-fforest. This is Pengam's garden village built in 1915 as a worker's paradise of five hundred well-appointed residences each complete with a decent sized back garden, bathroom and piped-in gas. Everything was white painted and full of health and air. It's

Peter Codling's *Mamgu*

worth a diversion simply for the history, the psychogeography of standing in the place where a great socialist idea began. Yet compared to the garden village at Rhiwbina this one comes off as far more cramped and grass-less. Its later extension built around the great green oval of Wheatley Place next door offers far more space.

Today, though, we avoid this two mile diversionary hike up the Monmouthshire hillsides to climb instead the slow western slope of Pengam Road. We rise through Penpedairheol (better known as Cascade) to reach Castle Hill near Glyn-Gaer Primary School. Locals call this place White City. Here the roads are named Oxford Street and Leicester Square although they still look like valley terraces to me.

Before the unexpectedly heavy-trafficked B4254 was built, Castle Hill was the main road. It's been reduced today to a council estate-style brick underpass, although, it has to be said, totally lacking tunnel trademark massed graffiti. Gelligaer, the ancient heart of which we now enter, is like stepping back into the green medieval past.

Ahead is the motte of Twyn y Castell, the castle to which the hill's name refers. Twenty-seven metres across and now overgrown and dense with trees as if human intervention had never occurred. Someone had a fort here: wooden and palisaded and now rotted; or made of stone and that stone now stolen, one or the other. The site is on private land and actually better viewable from the bus stop on the B4254 above.

The motte housed a Welsh castle allegedly built originally by twelfth century Ifor Bach as his high Senghenydd head-quarters and subsequently used by his rebellious grandson, Llywelyn Bren. History wavers here. Did the Marcher Lords ever capture this place? Before his death in 1314 did Gilbert de Clare's Normans begin consolidation in stone?

Bren, who was executed at Cardiff Castle in 1318, was buried not here, which might have made Welsh sense, but in the graveyard of the Grey Friars monastery in Cardiff. That's the graveyard that was mistaken for a plague pit in the sixties when excavations were underway for the construction of Capital Tower (then known as Pearl Assurance House). Bones and fragments of coffin were unceremoniously removed by white-suited workmen using mechanical diggers. Another Welsh hero's remains now forever lost.

Gelligaer is an historical vortex. Some places are. The poet Chris Torrance taught me that. "the stone / 1500 years a vibrant node / accumulating wind and water power / sun power /earth power[28]" he wrote in *The Magic Door*. He lived north of here in a cottage initially without running anything two fields from the road, on the far side of the Beacons. If you wrote to him your letter would be delivered to an upended mower grass catcher under a hedge. Alfred Watkins, to whom Torrance deferred but can be anathema to many academics, suggests in *The Old Straight Track*[29] that the lines of ancient power that girdle this planet cross and where they cross are often knolls and mounds at which assemblies would be held. Castle Hill is clearly one.

Here in the relict landscape is a point where the past laps and overlaps. First Mesolithic, then Neolithic, then Bronze age, then Roman, then early Christian, then Norman, and then finally the princely and still present rebellious Welsh. As you rise up the road from the remains of Bren's wooden fort, if remains they be, the wreckage of the past unwraps around you.

The Baptists are to the left in the presence of Horeb. Built in 1848 by the poet John Jenkins on the site of a smithy it was barely large enough to contain its 270 worshipers. The Baptists were strong in Gelligaer. Central entrance on a plain frontage, non-conformist lack of decoration, grade two listed but falling to pieces like a Jenga tower.

Further up towards St Cattwg's Church where the post office once was is the Twisted Ink Tattoo and Piercing Studio. It's a sign of modern times. Out back are a tumble of sheds done out as beach huts with the words 'Rum Bar' and 'Babe Cave' engraved across their doors. The church, St Cattwg's, is discernibly wearing away. Evidenced by Ogham-inscribed stones dug near the graveyard it was founded in the fourth century although its first recorded priest dates from 1266.

Today the render on its northern face is crumbling into the path below. It crunches underfoot. The mass of out of kilter gravemarkers show their great age by their moss-encased and weather-worn illegibility. Somewhere in this tumbling, overcrowded yard stand the memorials to a famous harpist and a gypsy queen. Amid the dew-drenched over-growth they're impossible to locate.

The church itself houses significant historical relics. An early Christian-inscribed stone showing a cross in a circle salvaged from Capel Gwladys out on the moorland; the village stocks; a full-body tiled baptismal pool from 1866; the Cardiff shopping magnate David Morgan donated the Lady Chapel screen. But the building, a refuge for the finding of God, is bolted against thieves and vandals, testament to the way things change[30].

John and I make our way through the gravestone maze at the church rear to locate between churchyard and municipal cemetery the overgrown trail of the Rhymney Valley Ridge-way Walk. The fields we cross stretch between the Ridgeway and the Gelligaer Road on its way west to Nelson. They are green and humped, spotted with curly dock and dotted with gymkhana poles and half a dozen rug-wearing horses. This is the site of Gelligaer's real historical wealth. Under this thin and categorically unflat veneer of grassland lie the remains of a whole Roman Fort: baths, tribune houses, workshops, stables, parade ground, granaries, barracks and practice camps. The extent is considerable.

Led by John Ward, keeper of the Cardiff Museum, the whole site was comprehensively excavated by the Cardiff Naturalists Society in 1899. Inscribed stones discovered date the fort to AD 103. The finds, lifted from their two millennia of underearth slumber, were often amateurishly jumbled, badly recorded and unforgivably damaged. But the site uncovered was considerably more than simply impressive.

Gelligaer, remains of Roman fort

If this were Knossos in Minoan Crete and Ward were fabricator Sir Arthur Evans[31] the world would now be parking their tour buses in the Gelligaer carpark and the Harp Inn would be serving like fury. Hoards would wander among the extensive remains, the footings and pathways, the statues and the restructured walls. The church would charge admission. Bren's castle mound would host conventions. Harp festivals would play in pavilions built on the fields beyond. The Neolithic common onto which we will soon step would host extensive tours. Traders would flock. Hotels would rise. As it was, and after a few photographs had been taken, the Edwardian amateur archaeologists were persuaded to re-cover their momentous discoveries and return the fields to agricultural use. The land was re-turfed. Today the bumps and furrows of the momentous past are celebrated with a bilingual plaque and a single interpretation board installed by the local authority. Their listed website is unreachable.

Traditional country walkers more used to stile and field than the Briggs and Finch urban rambler approach to valley discovery can now continue along the Ridgeway, waymarked for the next two miles, to Capel Gwladys on the undulating and wind-filled grass flats of Gelligaer Common. John and I have not finished with urban Gelligaer yet.

We follow Rectory Road out onto the B4254 to pass a plaque marking the site of Edward Lewis' first school (years ahead of its time for an industrial valley setting, capacity fifteen boys, constructed with stone filched from the Roman fort, opened 1729) and the splendid mash-up on the engraved name plate of the village hall – 'NEUADD KELL Y GAER 1911'. Signboard atrocities committed by Language Act-following local authorities are no new thing.

Gelligaer Square is where St Cattwg's faces down the Harp Inn and the Gelligaer chip shop languishes in the background. Here Rachel Fenner's Celtic mosaic centre-piece has fared only slightly better than her intervention at Ystrad Mynach. Locals have fronted this installation with another historical interpretation panel. Better than nothing but only just.

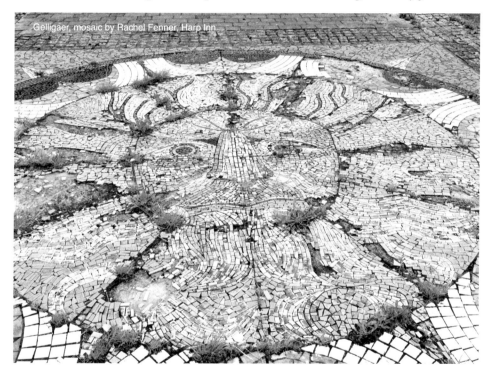

Gelligaer, mosaic by Rachel Fenner, Harp Inn

We loop downhill to curve along Aneurin Bevan Avenue which marks the southern extremity of a newish housing estate. Almost every house is the same as the one next door, apart from two I spot clad in stone-slab laminate and, for reasons I've yet to work out, both embellished with large wooden bears in their front gardens. There's light and air but a slightly Soviet feel to the sheer repetition.

There are notices saying No everywhere. To the expected council installed NO BALL GAMES signs have been added a run of 'SAY NO TO THE ALLOTMENTS' and, with slightly more frequency, 'STOP THE QUARRY EXPANSION – WE DON'T WANT ANOTHER TWENTY YEARS OF CONTINUOUS BLASTING HERE'. Untangling these two protests by talking to locals reveals that the quarry is further to the south and currently used by the Bryn Group on contract to the local authority as a landfill site. The blown plastic waste, dust and odours thus encouraged are proving intolerable. The allotments are a line of fifty or so to be sited by the same operator precisely to the rear of every Aneurin Bevan Avenue property. Would you like someone else's beans and compost heaps replacing your countryside view? Me neither.

Back on the B4254 Lyn Date guides his flock of twenty-five geese expertly from his farmyard into a field which once housed a Roman fort. His gate is secured with a padlock which keeps his birds safe from escape at the hands of forgetful Roman history thrill-seekers. He's farmed here for generations and can recall days when the shopping big city was Bargoed, the council estate didn't exist and the main road his geese have just waddled over was a mere track.

You can look south, back down valley from here, and above the trees see the peak of Malcolm Robertson's Observatory on the heights of Penallta Park. The south Wales Valleys may seem culturally distinct from each other, as they often are, but they also lie cheek by jowl. Nothing is far from anything else. Not really. Put your hand out from the Cynon and you can wash it in the Taff. We head on for the Roman road and the rippling Rhymney.

The Cross Inn stands at the head of Heol Adam. 'Full English Breakfast. Horses and Dogs Welcome.' Worth a break which we take. Last sustenance before Gilfach. Heol Adam follows the line the Roman road took. Straight and straight again out along hedged fields and then the hedgeless expanse of Gelligaer Common.

> The cold Roman grasslands of field hedge become field edge
> then no hedge, proud bracken,
> rattled, wavering, thistle, gorse, rush
> a concourse of unseamed horizon.
> a cloud roll, a half wall, broken,
> a tumbled wall, a grassed roll
> a cloud tree, a half wall, a hedgeless edge
> grass pampering rock
> humped and giddy to the horizon.

The land plateau here, bounded loosely by two Taffs and the Rhymney, rises slowly north towards the iron belt of Dowlais, Tredegar and Blaenavon. The grassland is scuffed with patches of gorse, fern, thistle and rush. The furze and bracken rippling as if this were Hardy country rather than the land of Jack Jones and Ron Berry infilled between two sets of great industrial valleys.

The common is empty of artificial structure bar the excavated rock heaps that are Hanson's aggregate quarry. The scars of pit tip and mining waste are mostly greened. The land would be empty if not for an interlacing of rolling roadways running from here to Bedlinog and Fochriw and Merthyr. They are ridden constantly by darting joyriders rushing east or west from one valley to another.

Our path along the now boundaryless tarmac rises and falls as if this were some vast fairground ride with only bird-call as music. Ahead is the knobbed Celtic cross pillar head that marks the site of Gwladys' ancient chapel.

Gwladys was the daughter of Brychan, King of Brychein-iog in the great post-Roman expanse of the uncertain dark age centuries. Myth, Arthurian invention, and conflicting lives of the saints suggest a life begun in battle but ended in beatific hermitage. Gwladys married Gwynllyw. Both became saints. His meditational retreat for the seeking of forgiveness was at Stow Hill in Newport. Hers was here on the bleak moors where she founded a chapel.

Caerphilly Council's engraved interpretation stone suggests an eighth century origin. The Celtic cross refers to 450 AD. North of here scratched across the moorland wastes are bronze age standing stones, ring cairns, medieval house platforms, Celtic field boundaries, post-Roman inscribed burial markers and the routes of ancient trackways. The soil is poor, the climate bleak and industrial interference far less than on the lands below. The past remains.

Gwladys' chapel is marked out by low present-day kerbing. The cross, its dominant feature, is of recent origin. The wind whips. Atmos is strong.

To the east of the road is a rough line of earthworks. These are what's left of the Roman Governor, Julius Frontius' practice camps where legionnaires were kept in trained trim by digging dummy forts out on the moors. Build it, have it checked, knock it down and then build it again. John shoots through the rib cage of a sheep carcase creating an abundantly green version of the Texas badlands on the south Welsh hills.

The road finally reaches the upper western edge of Bargoed where Bargoed Golf Course touches Heolddu Comprehensive. Among houses again we track downhill along the southern edge of Bargoed Park to eventually cross Gilfach Street beside the looming Edwardian bulk of the Capel Hotel[32]. This was the venue for the after plaque unveiling bash referred to on page 58.

The aim now is to locate Gilfach Fargoed rail station. East of here, downhill, by the river along valley bottom. This minute halt on the line between Rhymney and Penarth is barely long enough to contain a single coach and conductors have to arrange for arriving and departing passengers to use the front doors only. Locals refer to the station as Bargoed International. Access is down Angel Lane, following a much-weathered British Rail-era station indicator attached to a lamp post.

The single passenger on the platform, waiting for the next TfW south opposite a large 'Do Not Alight Here' sign tells me that the distinct entities of Bargod (drop the e) and Gilfach meet just uphill between the Capel and Morrisons. There's a new ticket machine still shrouded in packaging sitting across the tracks on Platform One. Sign of investment. The future in Gilfach is bright.

We are on the edge here of Bargoed Woodland Park. Before catching the train south and ending this six and a half mile adventure it's worth investigating Robert Koenig's wooden totems which stand at the head of a short forested slope. Here the Manchester born sculptor has carved three images of miners and set them atop four metre high poles. One each for the three pits that made this place – Gilfach, Britannia and Bargoed. The rough-hewn figures face in the direction of their collieries. Graffiti is little evident, just the rot of time among the fibres of the wooden helmets and the wooden heads.

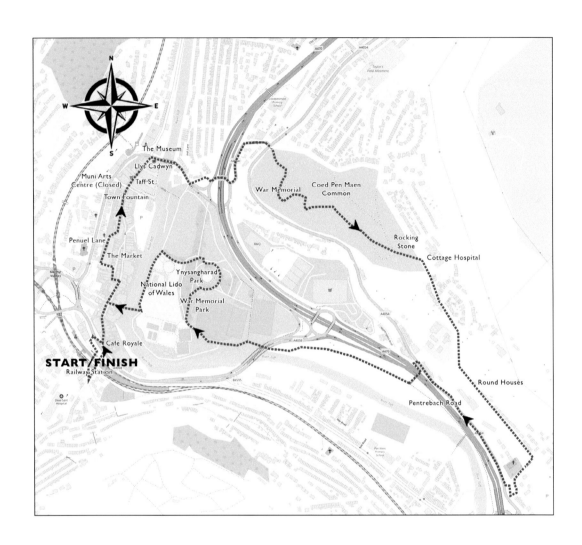

PONTYPRIDD

3.36 miles
www.plotaroute.com/route/973398

Is this Welsh Klondike a frontier town? Gateway to the Valleys, as the railway operators had it. The People's Republic of Ponty. Capital of the hill country. The place where the Valleys start. The place where the valleys end. This town of 33,000 situated half way between Cardiff and Merthyr has a rich history and has been called all of those things.

Its rail station, often claimed to be the longest in the industrial world, seems to go on for miles. As with most parts of the present day rail network this place was once a much grander one. Its shape derives from valley geography, little available width, lots of length. It's actually more like two stations built end to end and therefore large enough to accommodate the hundreds of passenger trains and races of coal trucks that once went through here daily. It's still busy enough but a shadow of what it was. We're meeting historian and Ponty expert Daryl Leeworthy who has offered to take us to parts of Ponty we might otherwise miss. He is waving from the opposite platform.

Pontypridd station platform

THE TOWN

Within thirty seconds we are deep into a discussion about the Arts and Crafts style Clarence Hotel which stood opposite until recently. This Edwardian structure was a dominant presence in Station Square, that triangle of what's called The Tumble that greets anyone arriving by rail. It was, that is, until the bulldozers arrived in summer 2021 to replace it with a new hotel. By the time you read this it should be up.

Most pictures of old Ponty taken here show the structure as The Clarence Hotel of 1912. Originally two buildings, the front part opened as the Royal Clarence Theatre in 1891. The Hotel was to the rear on High Street. Theatre design was based on the Prince of Wales in Cardiff, although perhaps a little less flamboyantly decorated. Flickering fortunes over the years had the original building do time as the County Cinema, Angharad's Tavern, a nightclub and finally an Indian restaurant. In its prime as a hotel it had caged monkeys in the bar for the amusement of its clientele, something its replacement no doubt won't be emulating.

The World Champion Lightweight boxer Freddie Welsh who had fought Jim Driscoll and controversially won before a crowd of 10,000 at the American Skating Rink in Cardiff in 1910 trained around the back here. Punters could come in to watch if they paid a small fee. Until the wall came down there was a battered blue plaque high up on the Sardis Road side which Daryl proudly recalls. Daryl has theories about Welsh's connection with Scott Fitzgerald and how he may well have been the inspiration for Jay Gatsby the title character in Scott Fitzgerald's 1925 novel, *The Great Gatsby*. It's plausible and adds to the town's exotic past.

Jacketless and with his striped jumper as proof against the impending rain, Daryl carries barely a trace of the valleys in his voice which belies his Ynysybwl upbringing and Ponty residency. His enthusiasm for his subject flows around us in a non-stop rush of fact and speculation. The Tumble across which we have just walked is lined with pubs. Five in a row, as good as you'd get in Bute Street during its heyday. Once known as The Criterion, The Bunch of Grapes, The White Hart, The Half Moon and The Greyhound today they are The Tumble Inn, Players, The Skinny Dog, The Soul Suite and Platform 11. Daryl has a theory that the road is known as The Tumble because that's what visitors to its taverns usually ended up doing. A Ponty red light tumble. I'm not so sure.

We cross opposite a sign reading 'Croeso i chick n land, Pizzas and kebabs a speciality', and according to the hand-written notice cellotaped to the window currently closed, and head down High Street. In some senses High Street as a street is a fiction as most of it sits on a bridge over the Rhondda River which storms its way south beneath us. We pass the Café Royale, run by the Orsi family and with pictures of both Bardi Castle and Pontypridd's Bridge in its windows. Their chalk board offers a two course lunch roast beef, tart & custard £9. The key structure here, says Daryl, is the former Butchers Arms Hotel on the corner of the lane which runs into the park. You can see its name high up in the gable. It's a branch of HSBC today but in the 1870s Pontypridd RFC had their HQ here. It was also the venue for the inquest into the 1856 Cymmer Colliery disaster. Behind stood the Park Cinema.

Among the parked delivery trucks and endless white vans it takes me a while to work out that this part of Pontypridd is actually pedestrianised, unusual for a valley town. Most are full of zooming traffic and uncrossable by-passes. The square formed by the meeting of High Street, Mill Street and Taff Street is decorated with benches[33] formed in the shape of anchor chains, recalling Brown Lenox Chain Works' significance in Ponty's history. There are words carved into the paving slabs. Fragments of songs, bi-lingual poems, contributions from schools and the memories of locals. Collectively it reads a bit like a David Bowie cut up from his *Low* period although I don't think it was designed like that.

Pontypridd, capital of the Valleys, the market centre of the Rhondda and the Cynon, the Taff and the Clydach. A town with civic status originally ringed by collieries close enough to provide the cash flow but far enough out to keep the dirt back. Name them – Great Western, Maritime, Maritime Level, Pontypridd, Pwll Gwaun, Lan, Barry Rhondda, Ty Mawr, Victoria, and Albion – all of them gone.

In early days the town was known as Pont y Tŷ Pridd, the bridge by the earth house. This became Newbridge after William Edwards built his arched crossing in 1756. Since 1856, however it's been formally Pontypridd, to avoid confusion with the other Newbridge in the Ebbw Valley and the dozens more scattered across the UK. Someone out there decides these things but inevitably the people who live in the place never get to vote.

We turn into Market Street where the market, the most well known in the Valleys, still flows out of its hall to fill the local pavements with commerce and bustle. Here you can buy glass elephants from a turbaned Sikh or iced cockles from a man shrouded in cap, gloves and hood. Elsewhere are carpets, cushions, towels, dolls, cigarette lighters, knee supports, toe clippers, screw drivers, super glue, filter tips, gas, grinders, pots, lollipop moulds, tobacco pouches, bri-nylon trousers, cable-knit cardigans and Christmas socks. To our right stands what was once Evans Department Store, the only shop in the entire valley area with its own lift and this one operated by a uniformed bell boy.

Within the rambling Market Hall entered from Church Street ahead the variety of produce on offer continues, valiantly fighting against superstore and Amazon, with offers of baby clothes, picture framing, net curtains, cameras, and a dart retailer offering t-shirts emblazoned with another of Ponty's claims to fame, the national anthem.

At InterBooks or Organic Books, two thoroughly thrilling and thoroughly packed second hand book stalls that roll into one, owner Simon Davies sells me a copy of early-years Anglo-Welsh romance writer Allen Raine's On *The Wings Of the Wind* in a Leisure Library edition for £1.50. I buy this not for the advertised "intensely human story" but for the

costumed, hook-nosed and gnarled Welsh witch depicted on the period (1903) cover.

We stop for a tea break at Cortile Coffee. Cortile means courtyard in Italian and 'Courtyard' was the stall's original name until the Marriott Hotel chain which operates an in-house coffee bar under the banner 'Courtyard' complained, threatened legal action, and then got their way. The tea is great. Daryl explains some of the Market Hall's origins. We are actually now sitting below the Municipal Hall, an abandoned cinema, reputedly still full of original moth infested seats and dust riddled screen above. Health and Safety closed it and it remains firmly padlocked.

When we exit the market onto Penuel Lane where Ponty's first Synagogue stood, a brief diversion to our left gets us to the rusted corrugated entrance to the original cinema. A set for a valley's black and white film noir if I ever saw one.

The lane returns, passing the site of the now demolished Penuel Chapel and graveyard, to Taff Street. Here stands the canopied, Celtic interlaced and four-bowled town fountain of 1895, restored in 1981 but still not serving water. There's a single Peruvian-looking Red-Indian-feathered pan pipe player tuning up as we pass. As I snap the fountain a white-haired gent approaches, poses next to it, and shouts "I'm old, too". I know the feeling well.

The spirit of unconventionality, deep in the Welsh character and a strong component of the make-up of both the literary forger Iolo Morgannwg and the promoter of public cremation Dr William Price still runs strong here. Both Price and Williams had Pontypridd connections. Their eccentric ghosts still ramble the town's streets (for more on both see the section on Pontypridd Common on page 106). In the next one hundred metres we are accosted by a *Big Issue* seller in a business suit with a lapel badge reading 'Stop Me And Buy One', wax jacket-wearing sixty-year old claiming to be a lawyer for the Kray Brothers, and then by a white-bearded wild man wearing a t-shirt which proclaims him to suffer haircuts only once annually and then only for charity. John takes pictures. It's part of the job.

At the junction of Penuel Lane and Crossbrook Street just beyond Howard Bowcott's silver chain-link inspired street sculptures we meet the former Mayor. Unplanned, but Ponty is like that. Jayne Bencher tells us that Pontypridd is not the Valleys but the entrance to them. "The town is a focal point industrially, politically and commercially and one that's looking towards the future," she tells us with keen enthusiasm, despite the increasing rain. She is involved in projects to bring the Muni Arts Centre based at the former 1895 Wesleyan Chapel just up the hill back to life, and the redevelopment of the former YMCA on the corner here as an arts centre. Beyond us are Ponty's new builds, the bulbous new library and people hub, a structure loved by the young and hated by the old. This area will be an artistic quarter. The prospect sounds exciting and almost doable. When you read this check how far they've gone.

Llys Cadwyn, as this part of the three-building and very un-Valleys looking Willmott-Dixon redevelopment of the derelict 1960s shopping centre is known, offers another hat tip to the Brown Lenox chain Works. Llys Cadwyn translates as Chain Court. It houses Transport for Wales' new HQ in splendid red, orange and yellow stripes. There is also a new public car park and yet another bridge across the Taff. The restored Lido, which is on the far Taff river bank from here, is the most visited attraction in Ponty, Daryl tells me, with most of those attending coming from outside the area. The biggest public complaint about the Lido has been its lack of parking facilities. So in an ungreen solution RCT, the local authority, has built one. The Gas Road Car Park flourishes.

Just before the bridges take us across the sparkling clean river stands Pontypridd's Museum. Opened in the former Tabernacle Welsh Baptist Chapel it's worth more than a diversion. In fact the determined could spend an entire day here. The non conformist interior has been maintained, soaring Siberian wood and a towering high seat. A complete and still working pipe organ the size of a Cardiff bus. Cases contain Taliesin James'[34] harp reminiscent of the one carried around 1950s London by wild Welshman Hugh Griffith in Charles Frend's film *A Run For Your Money*; union marching banners; William Price paraphernalia; two 00 gauge rail models replicating the spaghetti rail junction that Ponty once was. To operate insert a coin in the slot. I do. Nothing happens. There are male voice choirs carved from wood looking like a case of giant pencil ends, coal drams, lamps, tokens, colliery remnants, celebratory crockery, paintings of the Welsh past, cases of the Welsh past, air of the Welsh past preserved in every nook and cranny. If celebrated valley author Jack Jones were a building this would be it.

The bridge, the William Edwards perfection of an arched river crossing, we traverse next. This is the emblem of the town, the object of eighteenth century beauty that many ignore, unable to see it clearly for the two lane rattling road bridge built feet away to the south. Edwards' 1736 bridge, the Old Bridge as it's known now, was his fourth attempt at slinging a crossing over the rushing Taff. This local stonemason's earlier three all failed in storms or through the sheer weight of the materials from which they were made. The fourth magically worked. The magic is actually in the six discs cut from the arch, not for beauty's sake but for simple weight reduction. Splendid though this bridge was, its arch a perfect segment of a circle, and painted by the famous including J.M.W. Turner and Richard Wilson, it was actually too steep for horse-drawn carts.

Not that anyone rushed to fix this. It took until 1856 for the town to build something flatter. The three-arched Victoria Bridge, constructed only a yard or two down river, opened in 1856.

THE COMMON

Our route goes over and up Bridge Street passing the Llanover Arms and under the A470 which pretty much blinds us with its noise. This is soon gone as we rise up

Coedpenmaen Road and then Merthyr Road to access the common. Up here the view leaps out to run for miles. Valley vistas in all directions. The Council have installed picture boards to explain just what you are seeing. A whole industrial heritage of south Wales on display.

Coed Pen Maen Common has been a site for elevation and uplift for centuries. There are stone circles here, rocks resembling serpents, menhirs, cromlechs, and the millennia-old rocking stone. At the northern end stands the pointed sentinel of the Great War memorial. It's well looked after, picket fence, gates, and paths. A notice board nearby shows a photo from the dawn of photography of Ponty thousands up here at leisure escaping the ravages of satanic industry below.

The path across the common winds slowly passing pre-historic cairns and stone alignments to finally pitch up at the southern end's famous rocking stone. It is recorded in the middle of last century that hand pressure would make the top stone shake but no longer. John tries and fails. I stand on it. Nothing. This is the spiritual centre identified by Iolo Morgannwg and later by Dr William Price as a place for their druidic revivals. Poetry was read here by bards who had marched up in procession bearing banners from taverns in the town below. Chartists, ironworkers, and friendly societies held meetings here. The heroes of the Tynewydd Disaster were presented their medals at the Stone. There were fairs.

Keir Hardy addressed striking miners here in 1893 and again in 1898. Where gatherings were required the Carreg Siglo, as the old OS maps brand it, became the spot. Ceremonies continued for years, poetry headlining in a way that seems to have been lost today.

Price would attend in full druidic gear – fox skin hat, bright green leggings, scarlet tunic emblazoned with letters and runic symbols – in his hand a staff with a half moon on top. Near the stone he wanted to build a hundred foot tower to house a Druidic museum along with a school for the children of the poor. His fund raising however never got him that far. Chartist and early socialist, Price worked as a medical doctor and operating a sort of mini early NHS did this in exchange for weekly contributions from the workers at the chain foundry below.

Operating completely in the Morgannwg/Price mould was a third eccentric, Evan Davies, a local watchmaker and lay preacher. It was he who designed the eye of the serpent stone alignment leading away from the rocking stone. He did this for his own inauguration, taking the name Myfyr Morganwg, as self-proclaimed Archdruid of Glamorgan in 1850. This role he maintained for the next twenty-eight years, upsetting local Christian non-conformists by attending the stone at the solstice to chant verse and engage in pagan ceremonials.

How much of the spirit of all this that remains is hard to judge. Climbing onto the Carreg Siglo I attempt to channel Price in sonic rendition but fail. The sounds won't come, neo-Druidism fails me. Next time, maybe. Try it yourself. Climb the stone and chant a bit. See if the air moves or the stars turn.

Overlooking the common is the 1911 Cottage Hospital, the perfect Edwardian mansion paid for by townspeople and local colliers. Today it still functions as the NHS Speech & Language Therapy centre and Lymphoedema Clinic.

THE GRAPES, THE ANCHOR WORKS & THE PARK

The road descends now, down Rockingstone Terrace to Craig yr Helfa Road and the famous and viewable from miles down the valley Round Houses. Two white-washed columnar gatehouses leading to that museum of druidic life that was never built. Sitting above M&E Metal Recycling which fills the air with the crash of scrap these buildings are another Dr Price memorial. A blue plaque on their walls celebrates the great Doctor's achievements. Price had Round Houses built in 1861 and although the mansion they were to lead to never made it they still look imposing enough.

The road slips on down towards St Mary's Church and the Glyntaf Crem, Wales' first and appropriately near the site of the great Doctor's medical practice. We do not head that far but turn back on ourselves at hill's bottom to return to town along Pentrebach Road, designated here as Taff Trail (N).

Ahead, on the roundabout at that point where some might consider Treforest to run out and Pontypridd to begin, stands Andy Hazell's 15 metre tall bright red *Unity*, a heavy metal sculpture the design of which merges rail, bridge and ship's bow in a metallic swirl.

If you fancy a brief industrial revolution diversion and maybe a pint then it's possible here to continue straight ahead turning onto Ynysangharad Road to find The Bunch of Grapes. We are deep in Glamorgan Canal and Newbridge Chain and Anchor Works territory now. Workers at both enterprises would slake their thirsts at the Grapes. This is a real ale tavern which has on offer at the time of our visit Golden Drop, Oak Angel, Verde, Yu Lu Session Pale Ale, Wild Beer's Bibble. I am beginning to think they make these names up. In the back garden is the Glamorgan Canal. Part of it. Locks 31 and 32, the lock keeper's hut, a bridge, and, a real rarity today, a few hundred metres of filled with water canal. The locks are in the process of restoration at the hands

Pontypridd, Andy Hazell's Unity

of the Pontypridd Canal Conservation Group. Further south is a short canal nature reserve, Nightingales Bush, which also still holds water. There are conservation group aspirations to reconnect the two.

Construction of the Glamorgan Canal which eventually ran from Merthyr to the great sea lock at Cardiff commenced in 1790. It reached Pontypridd two years later and finally opened all the way to the sea in 1798. A branch connecting Aberdare was constructed in 1812 (see page 36). The canal carried iron, coal and the products of associated industries. At the system's height there were two hundred barges operating.

Immediately south of this preserved section stood the Newbridge Chain Works, as it was known when it opened in 1818. It was here that cousins Brown and Lenox made chains for the British Navy. Their enterprise began on the site of William Crawshay's forge and nail factory, producing steel cables and anchors for many great ships including Brunel's *Great Eastern*, *the Mauritania*, the *Renown* and the *Hood*. That most famous of photographs of Isambard Kingdom Brunel, top hat, cigar, hands slouching in his engineer's pockets was shot here, Brown Lenox chains hanging behind him. The works closed in the 1970s and were replaced in 1987 by a trading estate subsequently centred around a branch of Sainsburys.

Our route, however, takes us back to the station by a more direct path. Just ahead of Wayne Mounter's motorcycle dealership the Trail crosses the multi-lane A470 to give access to a long thin southerly extension of Ynysangharad Park. Here the Council have installed a free to use outdoor Lifetrail of exercise machines that will pull, pummel and stretch the bodies of users in order to keep furred veins and excess fat where it should be. Away. None in use when we pass. A dog walker. A woman jogging. The park itself is a vast green space, as big as the town shops and rail station combined. It outdoes almost anything in Cardiff in its diversity of facility and sheer green unexpectedness. It was created on farm and allotment land owned in part by Gordon Lenox, the chainworks founder. He lived in the now demolished Ynysangharad House at the far end.

Speculation over just where Angharad had her ynys (island) is still about. In the artist Richard Wilson's print of *The great bridge over the Taaffe in south Wales* made in 1775 a couple can be seen looking upstream in wonder from a rock-strewn smudge in the river bed. That's gone now, or at least it's awash with flooding river when I go to check.

We cross the sports pitches. Pontypridd RFC played here from 1908 until 1974 when development of the A470 caused them to move to a new pitch at Sardis Road. Cricket, which is still played here as the distant Edwardianesque pavilion testifies, began in 1873 when the park was still largely Gordon Lenox's farmland. Ynysangharad War Memorial Park opened formally in 1923, paid for by local workers. The centrepiece is naturally the War Memorial. The fields of poppies and cut outs of soldiers strung around it show its continued importance here in this backwater of what was once Empire.

The refurbished[35] 1927 Lido with its memorial plaque to Jenny James, the first Welsh person to swim the English Channel, is nearby. Next to it stands an extensive children's play area with climbing fixtures called *Pwll Glo* and *Chainworks* in an attempt to hang on, just a bit, to the vanishing past. In the sunken garden there's a coal-filled miners' dram (donated by Big Pit). On parkland gently rising north stands the 1930 memorial to the father and son team of Evan and James James who wrote the Welsh National Anthem. Evan ran a woollen factory on Mill Street nearby while James became a pub landlord and ended up in Aberdare where he is buried (see page 34). The memorial is a stylish Goscombe John bronze on a double plinth. It shows a half-clothed man holding a folk harp (representing music) and a woman swathed in robes looking serenely on (representing poetry).

Most of the poetry I've spent my life involved with is deter-minedly unserene, but that's another matter.

We exit over the cantilevered (and quite impressive) Marks and Spencer footbridge, still called that locally, Daryl tells me, even though the store that it is named after closed years ago. Its bulk backing onto the river stands empty. The pandemic will only be truly over when it reopens claim some. Around it charity shops blossom.

From the bridge's centre we stare out at the spot where the Rivers Taff and Rhondda meet. A surface flicker, a gentle watery crease, that belies this place's status, in Daryl's words, as the most important spot in the history of modern Wales. "The Klondike and Silicon Valley of their day, joining together, at a point where the energy and raw materials that powered the world passed. Everything from the coal that went onto the great ocean liners of the world – including the *Titanic* – to their chains and anchors, to the coal that powered the Royal Navy and the Royal Mail, so much of it came from the valleys that meet at Pontypridd." That's an echo of former mayor Jayne Bencher's declaration that Pontypridd here is not only the gateway but the guardian of all that made Wales rich and important.

It's only a short distance back up High Street to reach again the station. Trains to anywhere in the world, actually back to Cardiff, twenty-five minutes on a good day. Pontypridd has been a wonder.

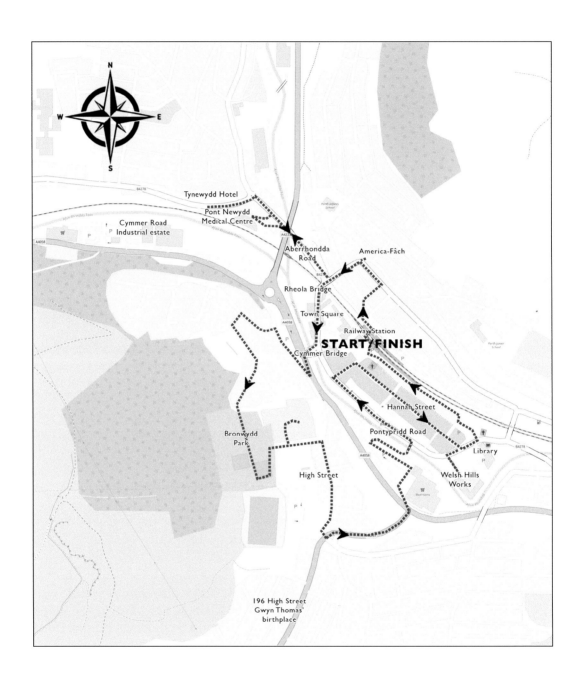

N
W   E
S

B4278

Tynewydd Hotel

Pont Newydd
Medical Centre

Cymmer Road
Industrial estate

A4058

Aberrhondda
Road

America-Fâch

Rheola Bridge

Town Square

Railway Station

START/FINISH

Cymmer Bridge

Hannah Street

Bronwydd
Park

Pontypridd Road

Library

High Street

Welsh Hills
Works

196 High Street
Gwyn Thomas'
birthplace

PORTH

2.81 miles

www.plotaroute.com/route/1000026

If any of the towns we are walking through could be said to be made entirely of coal then for my money it's Porth. In its days of triumph in 1913 as a prime extraction point for the British Empire's fifty-six million tons of coal annually its collieries were everywhere. Nythbran, Llwyncelyn, Glynfach, Ellis, Maesmawr, Porth. Dinas Steam Colliery, first pit in the Rhondda, is a mile and a half up the road in Dinas (otherwise known as Dinas y Glo[36]). And there are at least fifteen of mine owner George Insole's now abandoned trial coal levels up high on the eastern slope of Nant Colli. Cymmer Old and New pits were in the town's very heart, spreading their dust over everything.

It says *Porth* on the rail station signboard – 'Gateway to the Rhondda' – a slogan repeated on lampposts down the main street. Porth means just that, gateway, and gateways are important in the south Wales Valleys where there are quite a few. Both Llantrisant and Pontypridd, where we've just been (see page 136) are claimants as entrances, Treforest had a go and so did Taffs Well (see page 97) but somehow Porth's claim has more substance. With its high valley sides, the Rhondda alps shining, and its stumbling, subsiding terraces running in Gren-like twists and spikey turns Porth is a much better fit.

Like many places – Cardiff included – Porth was formerly called something else. In pre-industrial times Y Porth was little more than the name of a local farm. The first ever OS maps of 1833 call the habitation Porth Pont y Cymmer – gateway at the bridge of the meeting place of rivers – a hamlet near that spot where the waters of the Rhondda Fach and Rhondda Fawr come together. Kemer, it's been known as, along with Cumma and Cymmer. But Porth it has become. "Porth in the Vale of Glyn Rodeney", as John Leland[37] had it. The Rhondda starting to roar.

Porth, of course, is a name famous elsewhere. There's a 9.3k wide crater on Mars named after the town which puts Wales firmly on the solar system map. But, then again, there are also craters called Megan and Rhys on Venus and an asteroid up near Jupiter known as Dafydd ap Llywelyn.

We take the footbridge over the one-time Taff Vale Railway tracks, leaving the station's display of period posters behind[38]. 'Barry – For Varied Enjoyment', reads one, 'The Bracing South Wales Resort'. 'Porthcawl, the Children's Paradise', says another. Those, indeed, were the days. We climb the steep and swaying terraces. The climbs are prodigious with the pavements enlivened by sets of almost vertical steps reaching upwards at irresponsible angles.

Up here is a district called America-Fâch[39], Porth's one-time new world of terraces. They were built by coal owner George Insole, and situated where the town ended and the Rhondda wilds began. The name is recalled by America Place beyond which stands the highly derelict New York Pub and, just up the hill, the also derelict Gothic-styled St Paul's Church of 1886. The atmosphere is one of life departed, action ended, energy all gone.

Porth, Tynewydd Hotel and Rheola Bridge

Back downhill we turn off North Road to pass under Porth's version of Sydney Harbour, the arched bright steel of the 2006 Rheola Bridge. Visible further up the Rhondda Fach is the man-made, roof-like shape of Tylorstown Colliery tip. It sits there following us right around Porth like an evil eye. You look up and there it is, in the distance, glowering. Beneath the bridge is the Rheola pub complete with front car park and a pub sign from days when the brewery here was Rhymney and the trademark was a jockey riding a barrel. John, who has more strings to his bow than photography, has morris danced at the Rheola. Part of an annual Spring Valleys Morris Tour. Morris dancing gets you around.

We walk on up Aberrhondda Road to reach the derelict Tynewydd Hotel, a three-story brick and stone confection from 1907. The structure has done time as both La Maya Multi-Culture Restaurant and the Apollo Nightclub but has currently given up the ghost. It's been sold for redevelopment as flats but as that was more than year ago and in typical valley style nothing has yet happened. Things for the future look bleak. A local tells us that there's a complete nightclub from the 70s down there in the basement still as it last was when the then owner left. "This place is not what it was. You used to be able to buy anything in Porth once but now it's all fast food and crap," he continues. This is a theme supported by the state of this place where even the enlivening street artwork (football players, dancers and a 'Vote Muppets – you'll get one anyway' poster) are fading to ruination in the uncaring rain.

From few hundred metres on up Cemetery Road we overlook the sprawling Cymmer Road Industrial estate. This is currently home of Aldi, Lidl, Farmfoods, KFC, assorted wholesalers and a giant Alliance Carpet Mills. This was the site of the vast Upper Cymmer Colliery. Unmarked now. There's a van offering to give you 'Cash for Clothes', scales ready on the tarmac, at pretty much the spot where the first shafts went down.

Nearer, behind the Tynewydd Hotel where the space age Pont Newydd Medical Centre stands, was the infamous Tynewydd Colliery. Here in 1877 fourteen men and boys were trapped in rushing water and collapsing coal faces for more than a week. Five were finally rescued alive in an heroic operation reminiscent of that which brought out the Chilean miners from their Copiapo cave in 2010. The nearby Tynewydd Inn, now vanished along with the tramway that ran outside, was used as a makeshift receiving ward for survivors. The whole Victorian country was gripped. Praise was given. Albert medals were awarded. Coal had made its mark again.

Sunk originally in 1852 by the Troedyrhiw Coal Company, the Tynewydd pits finally closed in 1901. The Upper Cymmer pit, across the river and sunk in 1855, continued until 1940. Unless you looked hard at the angles at which some of the terrace fronts now lean you'd never know today that pits had been here, everywhere here, subsidence rampant, the ground below a maze of tunnels, shafts, drops, hollows, inclines and levels.

The route runs back to the town square that's not a square and, in fact, is nothing like a square. If it wasn't for the brightly advertised Squares Nightclub converted out of the former Post Office you wouldn't know you'd arrived. Here the buildings on the eastern side have sunk and are now at least eight feet lower than those on the west.

Any sense of Porth centrality has vanished under the onslaught of traffic arriving along the A4233 Lower Rhondda Fach relief road. We cross Cymmer Bridge over the rushing river, with care, and slowly, to pass the town's war memorial and then the Constitutional Club on our way to climb the valley's western side. We rise along Caemawr Road winding up from the hubbub of Valley floor to access the peace of Bronwydd Park above.

The park is the result of a land gift made by local philanthropist William Evans, one half of Corona lemonade and grocery business owners Thomas and Evans. His bust is on a plinth among trees near the southern gate. There he stands, half a smile beneath his stone moustache, stone rose in his stone buttonhole, stone tie around his stone neck. His park is a place in which the working poor would perambulate. Tennis courts, bowling green, toilets (with '#sexy' graffitied onto the side), lido (now covered). It opened in 1921.

Below is his Bronwydd House, now used as offices by RCT, the local authority. This is a three storey double-fronted villa built by local architect W.D. Thomas in 1913. Newman's *The Buildings of Wales: Glamorgan* suggests that this otherwise ordinary structure has been transformed by "the ebullient application of wildly inappropriate motifs in unexpected places". Pots, urns and heroic coats of arms along its balustrades. Its semi-circular porch has columns. One of its bays is surmounted by a sky reaching stone dome which looks like the output of a jelly mould. It's a fashion that has passed and right now shows no signs of ever coming back.

Downhill slightly we bear right and up again onto High Street. This turns out to be the total opposite of high, other, I suppose, than in its elevation up the valley side. We snake up to pass the slightly wrecked but still operating Cymmer Colliery Workingmen's Institute, then the tall frontage of the 1870 Cymmer Congregationalist Chapel, in use today as warehouse. Finally, at another great Rhondda multi-lane whirling road junction (this one built entirely on top of a burial ground, the victims of the Cymmer Colliery explosion and their Welsh-inscribed headstones vanished into the unchristian world), we find Capel Y Cymer. This is the Rhondda's earliest nonconformist chapel dating back to 1743. The revivalist Evan Roberts once preached here and the deacons on the big seat dominated the valley lands. The structure displays its antiquity with a long-wall façade which is how early chapels were generally built. However, evidence of significant vandalism is also on show. Thunderously cracked gable ends, rebuilt roughly to avoid collapse with contemporary brick and concrete block. Stone nameplate worn to illegibility, doors and windows boarded shut. The structure might be Grade 2 but on the evidence of what we see no one really cares.

High Street heads on up through Cymmer to Trebanog and the mountain top houses of Rhiwgarn. For those wanting a few more lungsful of valley air this is a worthwhile diversion. The views of Porth and the Rhondda Fach below are unequalled. The great Anglo–Welsh author, novelist, wit, and bon viveur, Gwyn Thomas' short story, 'The Pot of Gold at Fear's End'[40], offers assistance by advising the studying of *Through Breathing, Strength,* a guide to improving your durability in the face of heavy exertion. The walk also has the advantage of passing number 196 High Street, Gwyn Thomas' birthplace.

Porth, Capel y Cymer

According to the Rhondda Civic Society plaque Thomas was born here in 1913. His mix of dark humour, acid wit, working class political nous and valley history makes him one of the very best writers we have, not that you can tell this from current bestseller lists. Someone should start a campaign to regenerate awareness. It's massively long overdue. You could start now if you like. A copy of *All Things Betray Thee*[41], a tale of the iron industry's nineteenth century beginnings in these valleys, might be a good place. It's a novel of workers' uprising in breadth and soul. The start of a century and a half's class war that was never won. Unputdownable.

Returning downhill to the site of Cymmer Colliery itself, as ever, requires a quantity of lane jumping and highway ducking. On the hillside is a mobile butcher selling steak and scrag end. Up a lane a sign from some lost era advertises 'D A Davies Wrought Iron – Gates, Fencing, Patios, Stairs, Light Engineering'.

The site of the once huge and town dominating Cymmer Colliery is now occupied by Morrisons with its attendant car park and trolley racks. The passing of the pit in which 114 miners lost their lives in a 1856 explosion has not gone unmarked. At the side stands the expected dram and a memorial plaque. Looking out and up valley that Ynyshir tip still glowers.

Mine safety in the mid nineteenth century was not well regulated and mine owners were usually reluctant to implement anything that slowed down coal extraction. In the 1856 case gas which had accumulated in most of the headings was ignited by the naked candles miners used for lamps. The resulting rumble was heard as far away as Dinas. Today a disaster of such proportion would result in the closure of the operating company. In James Insole's case blame instead settled on the shoulders of his managers, overmen and firemen who were all convicted of manslaughter. Insole went free. Resentment festered in the mining communities for many years.

Crossing the Rhondda River bridge, the two tributaries of the Fach and Fawr now interlaced as one, takes us to Porth's Pontypridd Road. Behind us on the hilltop in the winds stands Trebanog where, John quietly tells me, he once had a fling. That was back in his student days when coming all the way up here from the big city for a night out might have seemed a good idea. "Does your wife know?" I ask. "Before her time," says John. Ah yes.

Ponty Road's blue-painted and refreshingly unwoke Empire Café demands a visit, if just for its imperialist-era name. Here, ensconced in the rows of sturdy booth seating, we have tea and toast. The owner in a housecoat charges us so little that I am afraid to quote the amount of cash that changes hands for fear of starting a stampede. It might be January but the Empire is still offering Turkey & 4 Veg at £5. Jam Roly and Custard extra.

We turn back on ourselves and into Hannah Street, centre of Porth's shopping flurry, and still filled with proper shops, sort of, cafés, butchers, a store selling beds and mattresses, phones, jewellery, kids' clothing. Half way down, if you take your eyes up from ground floor level (always a good idea), is an imposing four-storey Baroque stone and brick structure topped with a decorative rectangular inscription plaque. Its gold-filled letters read 'T & E 1905'. Thomas and Evans. Below are carved corn and maize motifs either side of what, from street level, looks like a frog. All further evidence of the partner's grocery empire.

At the end of Hannah Street before we pass Porth's bookshop (actually Howells Newsagents – three shelves of local histories, sporting memoirs, Vernon Hopkins' *Just help Yourself – Tom Jones* and a single copy of our *Walking Cardiff* which puts us both in a good mood) stands the boarded and derelict

remains of the Central Cinema. This is a movie theatre from the Valley glory days when a night out meant two features, Pathé News, a comedy short, and ice cream served by an usherette with an illuminated tray. An entire evening's entertainment which these days has been replaced by six pints of lager at the club while watching *Match of the Day* on repeat. The Central was opened by Solomon Andrews in 1916 and managed to continue showing films until 1966. After that it became the Palladium Bingo Club and then closed in 2009. Up for sale today if anyone is interested.

At the top of Jenkin Street stands the Welsh Hills Works, the heart of Thomas and Evans' soft drink empire. The works was originally opened in the 1890s and was where the two entrepreneurs created their answer to the temperance movement, Corona Lemonade. The brand with its wide variety of flavours including dandelion & burdock, raspberry and orangeade became a UK national institution and was sold door to door by deliverymen working much as milkmen did. By 1900 the company had 200 salesmen delivering Corona by horse-drawn dray. Thomas and Evans subsequently expanded to five factories and 82 distribution depots. At its

Porth, the 'Pop Factory'

height it produced more than 170 million bottles a year. The brand, Corona, which means crown in Latin and has no connection with the virus, was sold to the Beecham Group in 1958.

The Pop Factory, as the works became known, with its distinctive five story brick tower was redeveloped at the end of the millennium as a music centre. It was reopened by Tom Jones in the company of Kelly Jones and Cerys Matthews in 2000. They smashed a bottle of dandelion and burdock across its walls. It ran for more than a decade as a music tv and recording studio, music venue, café, and gallery hosting productions by most of the Welsh music biz. Times, though, always seem to get harder in the Valleys and much of that bright start seems to have faded. The site has been taken over by the charity Valleys Kids and now operates as a multi-function venue hosting concerts, training courses, parties, marriages and meetings. We have tea in the café sitting below a portrait of Sir Tom, this one titled *The Old Home Town Looks the Same*, and try out the toast. This time it's served the Cardiff way with a wrapped and frozen pat of butter, spread it yourself. Shame.

We return by turning left at the Library just before Rhondda Household, a shop in the style of earlier decades, which puts as much stock as possible out there in the daylight along the pavement. Here large hand painted signs advertise 'Curtain Poles', 'Work Boots', 'Quick Dry Paint', and 'Tanking Slurry at only £20'. We track along West Taff Street where the subsidence-aided slope of the terrace is quite significant. Lace-curtained front windows face directly onto the pavement. Many are filled with nativity themed dioramas. It's not twelfth night yet. Cribs, snowmen, santas, princes, wizards, snow-capped castles, stables, donkeys, rabbits, monkeys, and dolls form a wonderland of Frozen running right to the station.

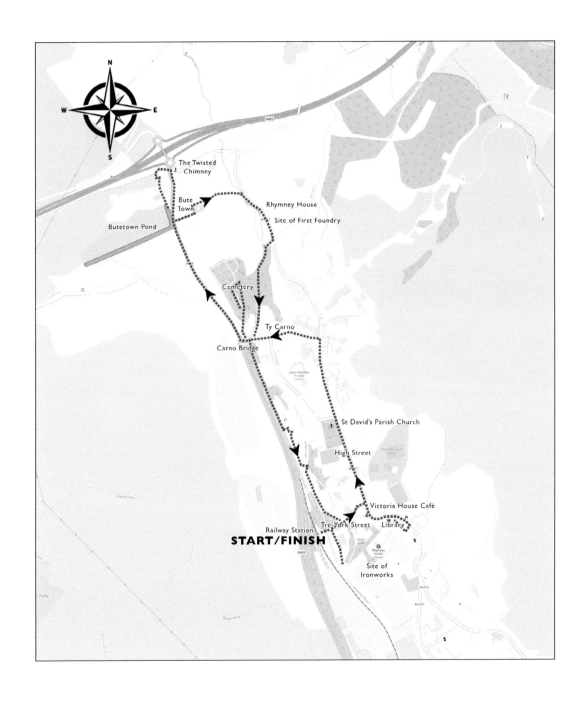

The Twisted
Chimney

Bute
Town

Butetown Pond

Rhymney House

Site of First Foundry

Cemetery

Ty Carno

Carno Bridge

St David's Parish Church

High Street

Victoria House Café

Railway Station

Tre-York Street

Library

START/FINISH

Site of
Ironworks

RHYMNEY

4.63 miles.
www.plotaroute.com/route/1647381

The line to Rhymney has been rising steadily now since well before Caerphilly. Maybe the air is thinner. It certainly feels cleaner as we alight on Rhymney station. End of the line again. A thousand feet up and the sun is shining.

There's space here. Rhymney's streets feel wide. A little like Tombstone just before the shoot out in the great Wyatt Earp western. Hardly anyone around and those who are sunk into doorways, watching. A teacher of my acquaintance working down valley in the big city of Bargoed says Rhymney is known to her pupils as Mordor. Middle Earth. Distant and dark. Although today in the February breeze it's burnished and bright.

The sharp incline from the station taking us up Tre-York Street pitches onto High Street, a north south terrace that's almost a boulevard here. Set back from the road opposite the 1906 Police Station and on a not that well cared for plinth squats Yorkshireman Michael Disley's sculpture. This is an Idris Davies-inspired stone carving of two workmen leaning back to back over a great stone bell. 'The Bells of Rhymney'[42], which the work recalls, was set to music by Pete Seeger and then turned into a world-wide folk-rock hit by the Byrds in 1965. Davies was born in Rhymney in 1905 and died in 1953, too early to enjoy his international success. Caerphilly Borough Council's public art interventions – we're still in that borough, even this far north – are generally well thought out and quite often uplifting. But not this one. It squats in

Rhymney, Peter Disley's *The Bells of Rhymney*

stained shadow. A miner and a steel worker depicted like garden gnomes and a bell looking more like a boulder than a thing that might ring.

Around the corner, passing the war memorial, is the Library with its collection of Davies memorabilia, photographs, the family bible, some of the poet's books and pens. Davies, the bespectacled Welsh poet who wrote engaging socialist verse, is probably best known for his sequence from 1938, *Gwalia Deserta* – the wasteland of Wales. These are poems of the pits and of pit disasters, of the General Strike which failed, the dereliction across the Valleys and of the great depression that followed. He was a people's poet. Accessible and memorable in equal parts. Still celebrated today.

His work has been championed by the late Nigel Jenkins who thought him nearer the people than most poets can ever get. Mike Jenkins, the Merthyr poet whose own present day verse is as accessible as that of Davies, is totally in tune with the elder poet. For both writers Gwalia is absolutely Deserta.

> The desert today is inside many,
> those boozers, smokers and druggies
> who stagger past the cemetery,
> cravings always digging deeper[43].

– says Mike Jenkins for whom all that's left of the old ways now is a "huge hollow in the hills where seagulls circle like vultures."

Davies, who started his working life down the pits before retraining to become a teacher, published three poetry collections in his lifetime. His *Collected Poems* came out in 1972. The plaque marking his place of death from cancer hangs on his mother's house a few metres along in Victoria Road. He is buried in Rhymney graveyard at the north end of town which we'll get to shortly.

The Library, a Lego cube architectural intrusion into the resolutely Victorian-looking Rhymney townscape, has an Idris Davies memorial outside. "When April came to Rhymney with shower and sun and shower" it reads surmounted by two columns of oak leaves and with the carpark and a further Idris Davies embellished bench beyond.

We turn back here to break, briefly, at the Victoria House Café, set next to sunbed centre behind the petrol station. The café is a breeze-block construction that is almost windowless. 'Recorded CCTV in operation' reads a sign in an attempt to be reassuring. The tea and toast served by Lisa with a Rhymney Valley smile, however, is fine.

Below the structure opens out like a Tardis to incorporate Jet Training Management cheek by jowl with Victoria House Leaving Care, a seven bed homeless hostel in a place you wouldn't expect to find one.

High Street heads north, thinning as it goes. We pass the Neo-Classical St David's Parish Church with its tower based on a coal mine's winding house. This is a Grade 2 listed structure created by London architect Philip Hardwick on commission from another big local hero, Andrew Buchan.

From Perth in Scotland Buchan came here first as the engineer who deepened and straightened the river to facilitate Bute's building of his ironworks. He went on to manage the Bute's truck shops. Truck shops were owned by many iron masters. In them they allowed their workers to purchase everyday items in exchange for tokens rather than money. The tokens formed part of the workers' pay and enabled the owners to profit not only from the employee's labour but their everyday consumption as well. Although they were outlawed by the Truck Act of 1831 the Rhymney Iron Company continued to run them for decades.

The operation here sold everything from groceries to mining items, clothing to candles and coffins to sweeping brushes. The Rhymney truck shops even sold tickets to the first ever performance of the *Messiah* in Wales in 1864.

Buchan's triumph, though, was the founding of the Rhymney Brewery on the flat land by the river, just down the hill from here. Buchan himself gets memorialised in the Andrew Buchan, a revivalist real ale pub built into a shop front just up from Tesco's on Albany Road, Cardiff. Good music most nights but a bit far for us to go from here.

The parish church architect Hardwick also has fans. He was a friend of the painter Turner and creator of the oldest extant railway terminus building in the world at Birmingham Curzon Street. He was also the man behind the now demolished Doric Euston Arch. His Rhymney Parish Church is on the tourist route. Buchan is buried in the vault. The graveyard, overgrown, closed, and with its rusted and leaning iron gates chained is full of swaying Victorian headstones.

In Rhymney the new is in scant supply. The town is full of what was. The Community Centre has a colourful mural showing smoking iron works, pit wheels, steam trains, and that hobby horse red-jacketed huntsman astride a barrel, trademark of the Rhymney Brewery.

Further on, just beyond the Rock and Rolls Sandwich Shop, is the house of Thomas Jones. Once a store it is now an unprepossessing, two up two down, street-fronting terrace, satellite dish, panelled and windowless front door without a number. 'THOMAS JONES CH LLD, Born 110 High Street, Rhymney, 1870. Died London, 1955. Founded Coleg Harlech, Chairman Gregynog Press, Deputy Secretary to the Cabinet. Secretary The Pilgrim Trust. President University College of Wales, Aberystwyth' says the plaque. How more significant can you become?

Jones wrote *Rhymney Memories* in 1938. In it he recounts the story of the place in the last decades of the nineteenth century. An iron town, owned by competing foundrymen. Rhymney had a company store, the former truck shop, which Jones ended up managing, a brewery, eleven chapels, two churches and a religious fervour that kept an entire worked to death population engaged, believing, and quiet. Chapels still dot the town but the fervour has diminished. Things here, as everywhere, are not how they were. My copy of Jones' book, from Gomer in 1970, is priced at £1.25. It is about the best Welsh local history I've ever read.

Rhymney is another of that string of iron towns that run across the whole heads of these valleys. Or ran, I should say. Not one still functions as an iron maker and most, with the notable exception of Blaenavon, have had their abandoned industrial remains removed almost as totally as the pits. The former iron towns stagger on empty in the high air.

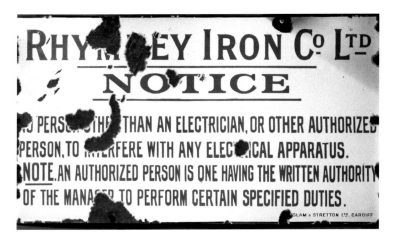

Iron making began here with a single foundry in upper Rhymney. It was fired in a snowstorm in 1801. It made iron for a few years before production shifted downriver. Foundry remains were demolished and, as was tradition, its stones scavenged for use elsewhere. The foundry was owned by

Thomas Williams who went into partnership with Richard Cunningham, Richard Crawshay and others to form the Union Ironworks. This was situated to the south on the east side of the river just below the present rail station. Bute opened his rival operation – the then futuristic Egyptian-looking furnaces of the Bute Ironworks – in 1828 on the opposite bank. The two huge operations merged in 1837 to become the Rhymney Ironworks. At their peak they employed more than 5000 workers. Today, as everywhere else in the cleaned-up Valleys, little remains.

We walk on up High Street to turn left onto Carno Street where far more recent houses face up with those from the past. Before us is Ty Carno, a former Rhymney Iron Company truck shop that well outlasted those Victorian days to continue as a general store until fourteen years ago. The present owner, Stephen Ryan, with a good eye for tradition and a keenness on restoring the past, has converted the ancient store to a contemporary residence with care. He's only too keen to show us round. The house is vast, a Tardis of rooms rolls on and back.

Former builder Stephen is also a collector. He has outhouses and sheds filled with Rhymney Brewery memorabilia along with a shining Jowett Bradford light van from the 1940s which he is currently restoring. His pride though, lies in his collection of veteran motorbikes. He owns a '68 Triumph Bonneville, a '53 Triumph speed twin, a '29 Triumph 277CC, and a '38 Sunbeam 230. He rides them all. Outside under a hedge is a half-wrecked 1959 Triumph Tiger Cub. Bought from a firesale and showing it. As a garden sculpture it's great.

Readers following our trail are asked to respect the owner's privacy here and not ring the doorbell asking for a tour.

When Rhymney was developing this area was known as Twyn-carno and was rich in early collieries. Twyn-carno, Tai'r level lo, Waun-Fawr, Bryn Oer, Gnoll Colliery and a variety of other drifts, levels and pits are all there, marked as *dis* (disused) on the early maps. The iron stone came mainly from the clays found alongside the coal or from patchworking in the surrounding hills.

Just before the roundabout at the street bottom we take the Carno Bridge to cross the infant Rhymney river. We are opposite the entrance to the Heads of the Valley Industrial Estate, strung back along the waterside on land once occupied by further coal levels, tips, air shafts, and the iron stone Nant-Llesg pit. Mining firm Miller Argent had plans to open a vast opencast site on this green rolling slope. This would have been a direct extension of their even larger operation at Ffos-y-Fran above Merthyr. Six million tonnes of coal would be scraped out. There would be jobs – good news in this jobless part of the world – but against a background of green revolt, closing coal power stations and an international reduction in coal demand plans were finally rejected in 2018. Rhymney breathed, those who wouldn't have worked there, that is.

Today the estate houses small enterprises with the expected run of seemingly made-up names – Budelpack, Celtic Foam, Convatec, Cyclax, Pakersell, Technical Product Solutions, TS Packaging, Pallet Express. The only operations employing anyone much for miles.

In Carno – now Rhymney – Cemetery and in low winter light we hunt the grave of Idris Davies. Rededicated with ceremony a few years back but still unsignposted and lost amid the mass of headstone and memorial. He's in here somewhere in the family plot, looking out at the slow green hills of Rhymney's valley head. Where is it?

A gravedigging team can't tell me. They don't know who he is. But Dean Hopkins goes the extra mile. Laying down his shovel he speeds off to consult HQ and comes back with the magic number. C518. We find it, the Davies plot. 'Hefyd am eu mab Idris Davies (y bardd) a fu faw ebrill 6, 1953 Yn 48 oed. Ni Caiff yn anghof byth[44]'. Bespectacled Idris tells it in *Gwalia Deserta*:

> The ghosts of a thousand miners
> Walk back to the streets again,
> And the winds wail in the darkness,
> And Rhymney sings in the rain.

The road is on and still up. Ahead is the small expanse of water now known as Butetown Pond but formerly called the Rhymney Iron Company Reservoir. It pulls the eye towards the green grey of Rhymney's top. Today the wind marks its surface with scrapes and cold ripples. There are no ducks. The Rhymney Railway once turned east here to reach Rhymney Bridge Station. L&NWR and Rhymney Railway joint tracks connecting Dowlais with Dukestown, Scwrfa, Sirhowy, Tredegar, Ebbw Vale, Beaufort, and the rest of the scuffed lands of iron. Today it's the A465, the Heads of the Valleys road connecting Neath with Abergavenny.

Mid-roundabout stands New York artist Brian Tolle's *The Twisted Chimney*, a sculpture based on the kind of chimney that would have been common among the iron works running across this strip of Wales. Tolle's £180,000, elastically bent red-brick stack is fabricated like Hardwick's Euston Arch might have been if Dali had been in charge. It stands, deliriously looped, as a beacon for Rhymney, its history and its slowly rising valley. It'll put us on the world map, declared a local councillor. Waste of money, responded Rhymney shop owners. What does it mean? What is it for?

Up here the valleys finally end. The river becomes a mass of thin tributaries. There is no more ironstone, no further coal levels, no adits, no bell pits. Instead treeless moorland takes Wales on to its green desert heart.

We turn back from the wind to explore Bute Town. Not the club-filled speakeasy land of my Cardiff youth but a model village developed by the Bute Estate in the 1820s[45] to house local workers. Initially these were iron men but as that trade declined increasing numbers of colliers and railway workers took up residence. Classical styled with Palladian

touches and made from unrendered local stone these sturdy terraces line up in three streets – Middle Row, Collins Row and Lower Row. 48 residences in total, pub, the Windsor Arms, St Aidan's Church, and a primary school added. Scottish style, Thomas Jones called it. In the 1970s following the failure of the then Gelligaer Urban District Council to have it demolished as slum clearance the estate was listed and renovated. A small museum (now closed) was added. The pub is closed too when we reach it although there are rumours that it opens after 7.00 pm and offers the best food for miles.

Bute Town, New Town, as it was first known, stands as an outrider to Rhymney itself. We exit Middle Row walking east through an ash wood to the site of both Rhymney's first iron furnace and the 1801 manager's house. This is now the Rhymney House Hotel but was once known as the Three Counties standing, as it does, on the meeting place between Glamorgan, Brecknock and Monmouthshire.

Despite its encouraging 'Open All Day' signboard the hotel is clearly not. It has seen better times. Its roadside barbed wire atop cold war era ferro-concrete fence posts does not encourage any notion we might have had for popping in for a pint. The ironwork furnace stood in the field next door along with an engine house and a few work-men's cottages. Today you can just about discern the remains of a block wall through the overgrown grass and the sheet of spilled slag that still lines the hill.

Our path winds on beside the river back to Carno Bridge. From here we follow Coronation Terrace to loop again across more empty land where industry once stood. This time it's the site of the brewery. Empty. A few crows. One woman walking a dog. The brewery still brews although not here and no longer producing anything like the quantity of ale it once did. It's now at nearby Blaenavon and comes complete with a visitor centre. It offers a chance to sample, a century and a half on, today's take on Rhymney Dark and Rhymney Hobby Horse.

Of the Rhymney Ironworks, the big one, there's little to see. The site of the Union Works on the eastern bank has been redeveloped as a trading estate and is full of medical suppliers, furniture contractors, car repairers, and horticultural consultants. On the west bank the land once occupied by the Bute Works is also vacant. It's a scarred, gouged place, broken rubble on its surface, buddleia sprouting. In a city it would be full of parked cars. Up here it's almost totally empty.

As a diversion, and not one forming part of our official walk, we check the former iron works' southern extremity. Here on a site once designated, rather hopefully I thought, as the Capital Valley Eco Park, are the rather anonymous-sounding K J Services Ltd. K was Keith and J his brother Jeff. It's a plant hire and leasing operation that also doubles as the largest graveyard for broken jcbs and other yellow-painted dozers, diggers, scrapers and pilers we've ever seen. A boneyard of faded yellow Caterpillars, Samsungs, Komatsus and Daewoo machinery stretches off into the distance, broken for parts, rusting in stacks, tyre mounds, dystopian heaps. It's the land of Mad Max, unknown and almost lost here on the very edge of once industrial Wales. Above on the ridge once stood The Bute Arms, centrepiece of Bute Terrace, an outlier of Pontlottyn, the next village south. Habitations jostle.

When John came here researching a few months back he asked a local if he could be told where the centre was. "We don't have no centres round here," was the reply. They certainly don't.

Rhymney, K&J Services machinery graveyard

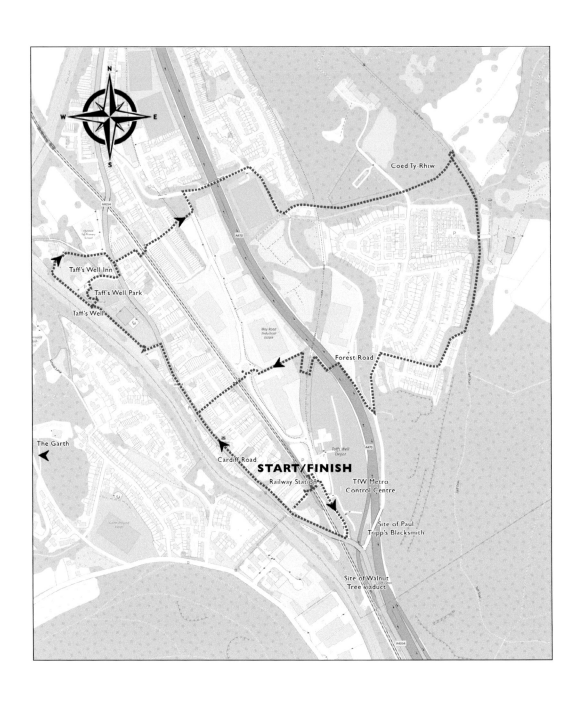

START/FINISH

3.24 miles.
www.plotaroute.com/route/1022154

In the cities traffic is on the retreat: bus laned, slowed, chicaned, bike laned, junction boxed, red–light stopped and banned. Yet here in Taff's Well, just a few miles north of the capital, the car is still absolutely king. Vehicles go up and down the main Cardiff Road like Gatling gun rounds. At the southern junction with that omnipresent Valleys feature, the A470, carriage ways swoop and spin. Here pedestrians have been permanently exiled, replaced by bollard, balustrade, and grit covered concrete apron. It's the world J.G. Ballard fictionalised brought to life. But John and I have arrived, of course, by train and, barring one short diversion, are soon away from all this.

Opposite the station on the land that was long occupied by the Garth Brass & Iron Foundry (latterly South Wales Forgemasters – a great corrugated iron sided enterprise of crashing fire and spark) total demolition has occurred. Even the Rhymney Railway sheds that hung on until at least 2018 have disappeared. Here Transport for Wales (TfW) are building their new South Wales Metro Depot. The current mess of groundwork schism and proud wound will be replaced by space for train crews, administration, maintenance, and a state of the art integrated control centre. Local rumour is that the trams are returning. I hope they are.

Taffs Well Station

We exit the large park-and-ride station car park south to mount the short slip road accessing the main Castell Coch roundabouts. Peering over a road sign (Ffordd Bleddyn) here and on through a concrete rainforest of A470 support pillars, safety railings, traffic direction signs, ivy clad tree trunks and revetment banks we identify the space where the blacksmith's shop of Paul Tripp and Sons once stood. It did so until around 1970 when its history, along with that of the entire Glamorgan Canal squeezing its way through the Taff's Well gap was swept to dust. The new trunk road north to the Heads of the Valleys demolished all that got in its way.

Paul Tripp had a single son (despite the plural in the signboard) and one who was never a blacksmith but instead a poet. John Tripp was an Anglo-Welsh rebel, and literary raconteur who died early in 1986 and whose memory seems to trickle through my entire *Real Cardiff* output as well as these present walks. Check the hunt for his traces in Whitchurch village in *Real Cardiff #4*[46]. His father, Paul Tripp's wrought iron gates made for the bungalows of Heol Penyfai still hang. They make a guest appearance in this present volume's predecessor, *Walking Cardiff*[47] and JT has a street named after him on the other side of the valley in Gwaelod. Let's not worry too much now about how that unlikely event happened but just note that his partner at the time of his death was a local councillor. But enough of shimmering air.

Further south are the two remaining pillars from the once great six-pillar Barry Railway Walnut Tree viaduct, a world wonder in these parts at the time, 470 metres long and another 37 metres up above the river. It was constructed in 1901 and demolished in 1969. One of the remaining pillars does extra time as a memorial to the Queen's Silver Jubilee of 1977. "A waste of public money," one complainant to Postbag moaned, imagining the pillars to have been con-structed entirely for the purpose of royal celebration. Today the pillar also carries a replica of the 'Cofiwch Dryweryn[48]' graffiti copied from the original on a rock at Llanrhystud in Ceredigion. This one more a stick-on poster than a sprayed original but a worthy sentiment nonetheless.

We turn back up Cardiff Road and head into what has to be Taff's Well's heart. Taff's Well, named after the well near the river (more of that later), is almost a Cardiff suburb but that's not something that residents like being reminded of too much. 3500 people are clustered in a place that long ago lost most of its heavy industry and is now virtually an outer district of the big city. One, however, with actual mountains and hills (including the very one that starred in the 1995 film[49] on the subject of how high a hill has to be before it is reclassified as a mountain).

Unlike most valley towns Taff's Well's terraces run laterally east to west. They are squashed between what was once the main road from Merthyr to Cardiff and the Taff Vale Railway. To the north there were collieries and coal levels including, up on Craig-yr-Allt, Rockwood - (old and new) - closed since at least the nineteen sixties. The town has pubs and chapels, a railway station, and one, single storey community hall (Owen Money & The Travelling Wrinklies coming soon) but no civic buildings of note and no real centre either.

Cardiff Road roars on, a thoroughfare filled with beauty salons and barbers, garages, and convenience stores, strung in line filling the only continuous north south space left beside the river. Taff's Well was the place where everything bottle-necked. An entire industrial heritage came through here. The river, the pack horse tracks, the toll roads, the canal, the highways, the railways: the Taff Vale, the Rhymney, the Barry, and the stuttering Cardiff. All found ways of winding around each other to twist through Taff's Well's narrow gap.

In its first incarnation as a settlement Taff's Well was known as Rhyd-y-Bythel, rhyd meaning ford. Mary Gillham[50] suggests that this place was at the southerly tip of a great glacial lake, dammed back up the valleys. The name of the next habitation north supports that idea – Glan y llyn (llyn means lake).

For a time the settlement was called Taff's Well. This was temporarily changed to Walnut Junction, following the name rather arbitrarily put up on the Taff Vale Railway station. It became Taff's Well again as the town developed. Today it's still called that. In Welsh it's called Ffynon Taf, absorbing Glanyllyn, and flying the southernmost flag for the local authority, Rhondda Cynon Taf. The border with the capital runs up the centre of the river. As a storesman in one of the builders' suppliers on the Cardiff bank opposite once said to me "So I can stand here, Cardiffian in Cardiff, like, and piss into RCT". He could.

A little before Cardiff Road rises to cross the railine and just beyond two houses beautifully named 'VALLEY VIEW' and 'TAFF VIEW' on paper nameplates cellotaped to the glass of their front doors, is a short track to the front of Taff's Well Park leading to the river. The bank, raised flood-defending bund, is muddy (muddier than anywhere we've covered in the Valleys to the north) but it does offer great views of the Taff in flow. In a clear sign of global warming the river flooded devastatingly in 2020, to levels never experienced before, with the bund completely overtopped with rushing water and nearby sections of the town thoroughly inundated.

To our left are the Garth peaks. The Cardiff district of Gwaelod hides in the trees. The site of the Pentyrch foundry blast furnace (named such but clearly situated in Gwaelod y Garth), all traces gone, is now the Heol Berry Estate. In 1840 a slanting weir was built here to divert water into what became known as Forge Dyke, feeding the iron works. Portobello, the weir's name, came from the now closed Portobello pub in Taff's Well which itself was named for Admiral Vernon's capture of Portobello in the West Indies in 1739. When the ironworks closed the weir was removed although traces can still easily be discerned, even at high water.

Just to the weir's north was one of Taff's Wells' ferries. The boat was rope hauled and moored on the Taff's Well side. If you were a Gwaelod resident wanting to cross you had to whistle. Today, making water crossing no fun at all, it has been replaced by a tidy bridge. The present incarnation of the Taff's great well is here, inside the park. To visit we leave the riverbank, cross the site of what was once the town's gas works, slide beside Ysgol Gynradd Ffynnon Taf, and turn back on ourselves to pass (or pop into for a brief break) the still very much operating and pretty ancient Taff's Well Inn. Out front are strung the flags of Wales, Scotland and Ireland. The Union Jack nowhere to be seen. This ancient pub was once known as the Rose and Crown and had a pub sign showing a man emerging from a well. When you came to take the waters this is where you stayed.

The well here is warm, tepid is the official word, and there is evidence that it has been in use as a cure for rheumatics and feeling dreadful since at least Roman times. There were five springs, originally, situated in the centre of Cae Ffynnon (Well Field) but the wandering Taff has done much to obliterate them. When the Portobello Weir was first built the river then actually swayed eastwards to encompass the entire well field. This left the village with a magic well somewhere out in mid stream and visitable only by wading to it at times of low water.

In later years various housings were constructed to contain the bathing pool. In the 1930s local authorities went one further and built a full-size naturally heated outdoor swimming pool to adjoin the spring. This somewhat overwhelmed capacity and didn't last. Today there's a Taff's Well Community Council blue plaque[51] and extremely boggy looking well house. Closed out of season (October to March) which includes today. As my gloveless hands have by now frozen solid (this is deep and crisp February after all) I push them through the well house window bars to feel the steamy heat emanating from the waters inside. Enough to defrost, slowly. This is Britain's Smallest and Cheapest Spa, as local promotion slogans say. Investigation in 1892 showed that well water came from at least 400 metres down and that the bubbles of methane gas within it could be lit. Although I consider it this is something I don't actually try.

John tells me about a book of Victoria-era letters sent from his home in Minnesota to potential emigres back home in Europe. It is titled *Bring Warm Clothes*[52] which is what John suggests I ought to be doing. I find a woolly hat in my ruck, better than nothing, and with both of us now looking like balaclava-wearing robbers on we go.

Cardiff Road, next to the Well Park, leads on over the rail link to turn Taff's Well into Glan-y-Llyn. Here stands Fagin's, a terraced pub serving real ale and with a long reputation for excellent food. Not open so we pass.

We head instead up Sycamore Street (NB no trees in sight never mind actual sycamores) to use the footbridge across the former Taff Vale Rail link which currently sends TfW units north to Merthyr, Aberdare and Treherbert. At Taff's Well station you rarely have to wait long. Our slow walk east up the gorge side crosses, in succession, the former routes of the Glamorgan Canal (now the A470), the Cardiff Railway, The Rhymney Railway and finally the Barry. There's little left to actually see beyond levels in the ground anywhere although the canal crossing still has a wooden sign reading 'TAFFS WELL LOCK' despite there being no extant water. The Cardiff Railway is under the Moy Road Trading Estate. The Rhymney, when we reach it through rising woodland, is now a walking trail, the track bed taking ramblers north to join the Taff Trail at Nantgarw.

Our target is the track bed of the once very successful Barry Railway. This was David Davies Llandinam's rival to the Marquess of Bute's Cardiff Railway. It directed valley coal away from the Bute docks at Cardiff to ones David Davies controlled at Barry. We pass the gleaming green grounds of Taff's Wells' football club with its stand named after Don James, the club president. The path now rises steadily with the stream, Nant y Brynau, at our side. We cross into Coed Ty-Rhiw, an area of signboarded woodland. Above us is the line of the Barry Railway, its track bed reused as the Taff Trail, and with the original railway bridges still in place. These are Victorian constructs of brick and are finely finished in masoned stone. This is the kind of decorative detail you'd never see on a railway today.

The line was primarily for freight but the Barry Railway took pride in its passenger services. It operated trains from Valley top right through Cardiff Clarence Road and on to Barry Island. Holiday Outing specials ran daily during miner's fortnight, the two weeks the collieries closed annually

Taffs Well, former Barry Railway bridge

for maintenance. These were the last week in July and the first each August. During these weeks the sands of the Island were filled with knotted handkerchiefs on heads, tea on trays and lounging in striped deck chairs. The beaches got so full that the council had giant numbers painted on the esplanade wall just so that wandering children might find their way back to their family groups.

The route is south, still among trees, Taff's Well and its TfW/A470 bustle well below us. Eventually a brown and blue city-style fingerpost directs us off trail and back towards Taff's Well station, although there is still quite a winding way to go yet. We are in a housing estate clearly designed by an architect who had not finished the course. Black fronted garages mar house entrances, gates face side alleys, slit windows allow in little light, roads bend and cross, as hard to follow here as the rerouted carriage ways set up to accommodate TfW's new build. The estate slowly gives way to wider spaces. Houses are larger. They have porches, hanging baskets, shrubs in pots, driveways.

Forest Road takes us across the A470 by pedestrian bridge and winds us slowly around the north end of the new metro depot to emerge at the freight logistics yard of Rhys Davies. The great Valleys author and the founder of this transport company, however, are not the same man. I explain this to a high-vis vest wearing depot manager who wants to know why we are taking photographs. "It's a conceit", I tell him, me being the secretary of the Rhys Davies Trust[53], and then go on to explain our whole *Walking The Valleys* project. He responds enthusiastically, on our side now, by talking up his hometown. Mountain Ash. "You should definitely include it. It's full of historical interest: Guto Nyth Brân and the starting place for the annual Nos Galan road race; Harri Webb; Elaine Morgan." Maybe we should.

He's certain of one thing, though. Taff's Well is absolutely the Valleys. The start of them, or their end. We cross the rail line on a pedestrian level crossing to find ourselves back on Cardiff Road and Taff's Well's only café which doubles as the Post Office. I ask the owner, Val Carroll, the same question. "Is this the Valleys?" "No," she's sure. "The post code is CF. Says it all. But then I am a Docks girl." Where Taff's Well is depends on your origins. In the straw poll I then take asking passers-by outside I get the same mixed response. Sometimes Taff's Well is the Valleys, sometimes it's not. What it usually isn't, Docks girls aside, is Cardiff.

On the long wall above the card displays in the Post Office café are a set of early Taff's Well photos. The ferry boat on the Taff. Shops that have been outlived or sold on. Marching bands. The well house. Faces of long gone residents smiling out through the black and white dust.

In this village I'm struck by how much Welsh-medium signage there is. House names. Shop welcome notices. Croeso I Co-op Ffynnon Taf. Dan-y-Coed. Glasbant. Cartref. Gan Brynu Yr Amser. Ffynon Dwym. Easy, friendly, and Cardiff Road excepted, wonderfully slow, unlike the city next door.

As predicted the train is there as soon as we reach the station and in 15 we are back on Queen Street where all that rush returns. There are just too many people to say hello to so you say hello to no one. Next walk is Valleys proper. Can't wait.

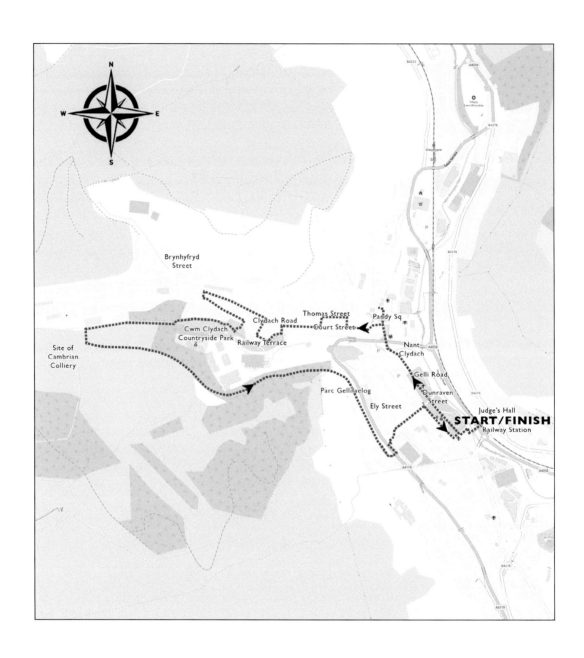

TONYPANDY

4.48 miles
www.plotaroute.com/route/877222

Over Queen Street Station the sun unexpectedly breaks through. The tea stall on platform four, now known with classic Cardiff overstatement as the Gourmet Café Bar and Kitchen, does a brisk trade. The rattle and roll on the train takes 45 minutes. Ten quicker we are promised when the metro is fully functioning. But not yet.

For today's amble we've been joined by historian Dai Smith, a year older than both of us but just as fast. He was born here, in the Tonypandy terraces above, where working-class history arrived by osmosis in his blood.

We've dismounted onto the same Tonypandy platform that the Lancashire Fusiliers left from in 1911 after helping quell Tonypandy's shop-smashing riots. The *Rhondda Leader* carried a photo of them armed and smiling with the Judge's Hall, opened two years earlier and as yet unsullied by time, towering up behind. Today the Hall is ragged, offering bingo in an attempt to put off the demolition that will inevitably befall it. In recent decades it's been the venue for the guitar-led rock of Man, the jazzy flights of East of Eden, and the heavy thunder of Black Sabbath. This detail is imparted by Dai Rock (that's his name, he insists) who greets us at the top of the station slope.

Not that any of us know Dai Rock but this is the Valleys and such things do not matter. Noting our ostensible interest in the faded music venue he entertains us with the story of local boy Gordon Mills who discovered Tommy Scott and the Senators and then managed their lead singer to world-wide triumph as Tom Jones. This tale morphs into one about Norman Wisdom in the film *Trouble In Store*, asking at a London station for a ticket to Tonypandy, the only Welsh valley name, apparently, that Wisdom could pronounce. The discussion rattles on to discourse on the town's various cinemas (The Hippodrome – later the Plaza, The Empire, The Picturedome, and one up valley in Llwynypia known as Dwts) and their ultimate fates – closure, all of them, and demolition when their empty shells present safety risks.

The route to town, considerably messed-about with since they built the bypass (a thing they appear to have done throughout the Valleys), is via a footbridge over the Rhondda River. Oily black when Dai Smith was a kid. "You had to change your shirt twice a week for the amount of coal dust in the air" he tells me.

We climb to access the bottom end of Dunraven Street. This is Tonypandy's main drag. In its heyday it was a rushing meld of store and shopper buying and selling just about any-thing you'd care to name, all to be carried home on the Rhondda tram[54] which rattled through here on its way up and down the valley.

But that sprawling victory for commerce is long gone. Today it's mostly boarded closure: carpet centres, pine dungeons, vaping outlets, pound shops, second hand stores, and tattoo parlours. The council's attempts at encouraging regeneration by the demolishing of rows of stores and replacing them with an ill-fitting shopping mall has not succeeded.

To our left, in the Trealaw direction, is a vacant lot where the Plaza once stood. With its continuously rolling programme of main film, B film and newsreel you arrived and left as it suited, often seeing the end before the start and still piecing the drama together. An early form of modernism according to Dai.

On the corner of Dunraven and Trinity Road, Trinity Hall has been turned into a private house. 'Zak's Ty Cariad', reads a sign. 'One Love' reads a second. Below that is one warning 'Beware of the Wife' and another announcing that 'The More I Learn About People The More I Love My

Dogs'. The remnants of a glorious past are all here. Eglwys Dewi Sant, the 1876 Police Station, the site of Tonypandy Central Hall, as mentioned by Lord Haw Haw in despatches. "It will be bombed tonight" he announced. Crowds of locals came out to watch. The Luftwaffe missed.

The central section of Dunraven was pedestrianised by the council in the mid-nineties to mixed results. Half way along Howard Bowcott has created an artwork representing the sandstone and coal strata below us at this point. Its sides are embellished with poems about coal, one from Menna Elfyn and the other by Gillian Clarke. High on Trealaw mountain in glaring white shines former painter and decorator Glyn Thomas's crucifix in a further attempt to set this town's spirit back alight.

We pass the Purple Leek, that John mistakes for a replica of the Purple Onion, the pizza café back home in St. Paul, Minnesota, from where Bob Dylan left to hitch hike to New York in search of Woody Guthrie in January, 1961. Turns out, though, that this piece of alternative culture has nothing to do with the American singer and is, in fact, a tattoo and piercing parlour with head shop overtones. The assistant tells John she has no idea who Bob Dylan is. This is a bit of a surprise, although we are in Tonypandy. Dunraven rolls on.

Tonypandy, as Dai explains, boomed as a pit town at the start of the twentieth century when coal owner D.A. Thomas, later Lord Rhondda, formed a cartel known as the Cambrian Combine with the Cambrian, Glamorgan, Naval and Britannic Merthyr collieries at its heart. The result, though, was a continuation of the much-hated sliding-scale of payment rates and increasing friction between employee and employer as the Combine, much like many mine owners had before, attempted to hold down wages to the detriment of the miners' lives.

On Wednesday 2nd November, 1910 a mass meeting was held at the Tonypandy Empire. Local photographer Levi Ladd took a portrait of the miners assembled up the incline of Gelli Road. This sea of hundreds of pale Dai-capped faces has become world famous. In the centre stands Dai Smith's grandfather, Dai Owen, an immigrant quarryman from the slate quarries of Blaenau Ffestiniog. His gaze is central on the souvenir mug the National Museum have now emblazoned with this iconic symbol of Welsh working-class defiance.

John recreates it, Dai holding an enlargement of Ladd's original, mid-road, Iceland to his right, Cwtch Comfort Furniture to his left, traffic on stop, posed just where his grandfather stood. Passing locals give us a cursory glance, little more. Despite its huge significance history here has seeped down the river.

The riots of the evening of Tuesday 8th November, 1910 took out the frontages of some sixty shops along Dunraven. Miners paraded through the town wearing women's hats, brand new shirts and carrying hams, rolls of cloth, legs of lamb, whole cheeses, and bowls of fruit, all looted in a frantic three hours of civil disobedience. These disturbances ultimately won the strikers little. But it was a battle that changed the course of labour relations and damned Churchill (falsely, Dai claims) as a troop-deploying English overlord and who, despite his World War Two victory, remains today a figure of hate throughout south Wales.

Dunraven Street rises towards Pandy Square. On the right where the Nant Clydach flowed into the Rhondda River stood the Pandy, the cloth making fulling mill, from which Tonypandy gets its name. Nothing to see. Rumours abound of remnants lasting to mid-twentieth century but they've gone now. Opposite, beyond the former Town Hall, on the edge of a car park, is the 1908 statue of the Lady of the Lamp. Silken robed female forms are a Valleys' theme. This one, hands aloft holding a globular light, was originally in Pandy Square and had a fountain and horse troughs attached. It was paid for by local miners as a memorial to the much-liked pre-Combine coal owner Archibald Hood.

Tonypandy, *the Lady of the Lamp*, 1908

Pandy Square itself is a huge disappointment. A shamble of roads and car park mixed in with waiting buses and blokes outside the Pandy Inn leaning on the wall fags in hand. The trams are long ripped up and commerce is at a minimum. Dunraven Street has given way to De Winton. Below us would have stood J Owen Jones' Pavilion Skating Rink where, controversially, riot-quelling Metropolitan Police, known as metro's, were billeted and Dr Tudor Morris (from Rhys Davies' Rhondda novel, *A Time To Laugh*) had his surgery deep among the seething streets. An "ugly black old house left derelict among the crowded terraces of the notorious Nant-Ddu district[55]". The Tonypandy Health Centre with its person-high lettering spelling the glorious word 'TONYPANDY', least anyone should forget just where we are, plus a splendid full town mural done by the local school inside, stands there instead.

A statue of Archibald Hood is still in place. It's a hundred yards on in a thin park beside the Llwynypia Road. Behind stood the now demolished Llwynypia Workingmen's Institute and Library. Behind them are the terraces, the sought-after Scotch houses built in 1865 for Hood's workers. Below, where the man himself stares with his bronze vacant eyes, his snow white trousers still carrying flecks of paint from their 1906 heyday as a man the people respected, is where his pit – the great Llwynypia Colliery – once sprawled in its blackness across valley bottom. Replaced by clean industrial unit and car park. Jobs for 10% of the number of colliers who once toiled here, if we're lucky.

But our walk sticks to Tonypandy, or Blaen Clydach as the map calls it now. As ever settlements merge, communities melt into each other. The novelist and short story writer Rhys Davies describes the place as a tributary vale of seething terraces. A sharp sided and tightly-pointed diversion from the Rhondda's north rising regular progress. As we turn in the light perceptibly fades. The pavement climbs and carries on doing that, without stop, right up the length of Court Street, then all of Clydach Road, to exhaust itself up beyond Howard Street where the tight streets finally end and the trees begin.

The cars here are held to the tarmac by magnetism. It is all that prevents them from toppling. While Court Street's rising progress is itself dramatic, on the many side streets things are histrionic. You rise and rise and then rise again. At street's top are hand-railed steps and above them more flights, ascending as if you are climbing into a house loft beyond which are even further terraces clinging to the hillside on their way to heaven. They hold on by a trick of gravity that only the miners knew. Now they are gone we all await the fall.

Below Court Street, a minor diversion for fans, is the plaque-bearing house where boxer Tommy Farr[56] was born in 1914. 3 Railway Terrace. The 'Tonypandy Terror', as he was known, controversially fought Joe Louis for the World heavyweight championship in 1937. Winning, many thought, but formally losing on the smallest number of points.

In fact the whole of Blaen Clydach is riddled with the marks the famous left. High up on Brynhyfryd Street is the house where Lewis Jones wrote his epic of industrial novel *Cwmardy*. Sunny Bank, where he was born, stood 500 yards west. The original has been demolished and a more impressive replacement built instead. Plaqueless. So far. But given Lewis Jones' enduring reputation who knows for how long.

On Thomas Street, running parallel to Court Road, is the house where the Houston brothers were born. An acting dynasty. Donald was born in 1923. Star of *The Blue Lagoon* and *633 Squadron* he is remembered on the Pandy Square RCT interpretation board as appearing in that Ealing comedy, *A Run For Your Money*, playing "a young miner from the fictitious village of Hafoduwchbenceubwlly-marchogoch"(See also page 104). Glyn, born two years later, had more than 200 TV and film appearances to his credit beginning with *The Blue Lamp* in 1950. He died in 2019.

Rhys Davies himself, one of the Rhondda's greatest literary sons, was born at 6 Clydach Road in 1901. Royal Stores in his day. His family of grocers lived above the shop with Rhys' bedroom staring straight out at the rumbustious pub, The Central, situated opposite. Both no longer trading. The house altered, the storefront turned to a front room, the pub closed and boarded. But a memorial plaque hangs above the house door.

During the riots of 1911 a terrified young Rhys watched from his bedroom window as battling men emerged the worse for beer from the Central. They set about each other with drunken vigour. The road was "crammed with yelling strikers armed with sticks and mandrels…. I saw a helmet flying on the porch steps of the pub, a rioter falling there, and a baton crashing down on his head as he attempted to rise." Rhys recalls this in *Print of a Hare's Foot*[57] along with the story of Esther, the west-Walian family maid, rushing from her room to lend a fighting hand to her rioting miner brother who was not doing well for himself at the time. The drama is rich, depth added by being able to stand there yourself and see the very steps on which blood was spilled.

Forgoing the Victorian terraced wonders: Georgie Price's outpost of a greengrocers, still trading all these miles from Ton central; the cast-iron frontage of the crumbled Bush Inn up beyond the Primary School; even the Marxian Club at 118 Court Street into which John had to be restrained from diverting; we turn down Brynheulog to access the

grandly named Cwm Clydach Countryside Park. This has been created from the waste land left by the Cwm Clydach Colliery and the rows of coke ovens which surrounded it.

Today it offers lake views, ducks, a café bar and a small outdoor pursuits centre. Kayaks thread their way across the calm waters bound for the single island on which they will not land. The lake has a twin a mile on up the valley on the site of the much larger and longer-lived Cambrian Colliery. On the way there's a moving memorial to the Cambrian in the form of the pit wheel leaning against a wall, a freshly painted pit cage and a coal-filled dram. Nearby are four finger-posts bearing arrows which show the precise position of the Cambrian's four shafts. In an episode of commendable green innovation the local authority generate power by allowing water to fall piped between the two lakes through a small hydroelectric generator. The Hoover Dam maybe not but it's something.

We walk on up valley, city boys pacing ourselves on the steady incline steep, blithely followed by retired often limping but still agile locals with their inevitable dogs. A short distance before the memorial we turn left through the trees to climb and access the track bed of the Ely and Clydach

Valley Railway, a broad gauge creation built in 1873 to carry the Cambrian's increasing output to port. The views from this valley side vantage point are expansive. The whole of Clydach Vale's seething self-confident townscape lies spread before us. Its myriad twists and rises, its houses braced into each other as they climb the impossible near vertical streets. We can see Rhys Davies' Clydach Road clearly as well as Lewis Jones' Brynhyfryd house from where he stared out at the mix of green valley landscape and coal black pit below.

The track bed runs east above Cambrian Industrial Park and the Rhondda Athletic ground. Bending south the terraces of Tonypandy appear below. Ahead is a new build estate of smart detached executive homes with double garages and conservatories. This is Parc Gellifaelog built across farmland that once bore its name. The Rhondda, after all these years, finally changing gear. Below is the overgrown Tonypandy Soccer ground and cycle track, the sports pitch where generations of striking miners met and thousands of spirits were raised.

We cross the busy A4119 that only takes a further three miles to get to Tonyrefail, to access Gelli Road which hillsides its way down into the town. It's steep but not a patch on some of the inclines we've just encountered in Clydach Vale itself. We pass Ely Street, a tight row of terraces but with something additional about them – bay windows, slim front gardens crossed by steps. Dai's birthplace. We take a look and have him photographed standing proudly outside. No plaque yet, you only get those when you are dead.

The slide down Gelli Road returns us to Dunraven Street, indolent in the sun. just as we left it. Pound Stretcher is still pulling them in while Tonypandy Army Surplus – Air Guns Tackle Workwear – remains closed. Its shutters are down as if this was Zinc Town post-riots all over again. The station is a couple of hundred yards down in the Dinas direction. Still Tonypandy but only just.

Tonypandy, view from Gelli Road

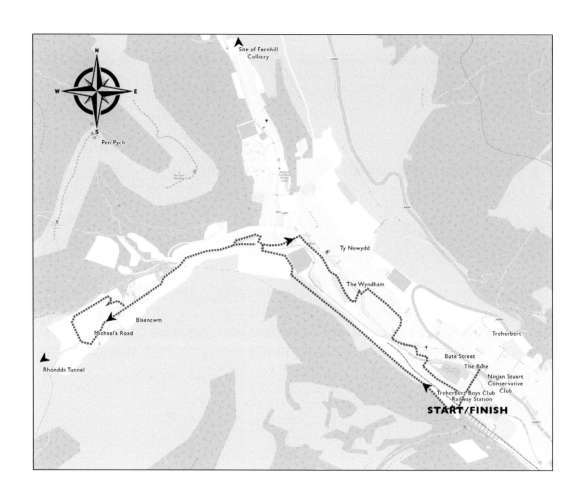

Site of Fernhill
Colliery

Pen Pych

Ty Newydd

The Wyndham

Blaencwm

Michael's Road

Treherbert

Rhondda Tunnel

Bute Street

The Bute

Ninjan Stuart
Conservative
Club

Treherbert Boys Club
Railway Station

START/FINISH

TREHERBERT

4.34 miles.
www.plotaroute.com/route/1081221

As it climbs towards the Beacons the Rhondda drops all pretence as industrial memorial to become a Welsh Cumbria or Glencoe or Switzerland. Blind valleys fork into rising treescapes turning to crag and rock with the spectacularly flat top of Pen Pych dominant central. Above mountain ridge the blades of giant wind generators slowly turn. In its industrial day this place was blacker than anywhere. Collieries and their attendant surface scarring on every available square yard of valley flat, the workers' settlements caulked in between like filler.

Treherbert was always Bute land. It's been so since the Second Marquess bought Cwmsaerbren farm here from William Davies in 1845. Earlier than that there were only a few dozen souls living in the entire valley head. Bute has made his mark. You can tell immediately by the grid layout of the central streets, their uniform two-storied single-fronted terrace construction and then the giveaway on the name plates: Bute, Dumfries, Stuart, Ninian, Crichton, all streets that are so familiar from other locations in Bute Estate south Wales. Bute bought the land, he funded the railway, he ran the collieries. His workers' houses were always solidly made from local rock. In Treherbert you gaze at the grey-brown Pennant stone of these structures and then look up to see the same material outcropped right along the Valley sides.

Treherbert is now the rail head. The trains once carried on through Tynewydd to Blaen Rhondda and Blaen Cwm. A single track continued through the mountain to Blaengwynfi and the Afan Valley on the other side. The Rhondda and Swansea Bay Railway, a connector between industrial outposts in the valley top world. But that's all the past. Tracks have shrunk to a single line and terminate at Treherbert's solitary platform. There is even talk, to save money, of the tracks retreating back down valley to Treorchy but nothing has happened yet.

Treherbert, Rhondda Fawr rail head.

Warning
Do not trespass
on the Railway
Penalty £1000

GROESO I
DREHERBERT

Beyond the ticket office, on Station Road, there's a house-end mural showing a diesel sprinter reaching track top. The hills are full of trees. 'Croeso i Dreherbert' the mural reads. Welcome to Herbert Town. No mention of the three Herberts that one local *Treherbert In Old Photographs* compiler suggests. The Herberts of this place are the Pembrokeshire Earls, Bute's regal ancestors.

What do John and I make of this town and why have we come? We're here because this is where the Welsh valleys end. Maybe not the final deep pit – that was Tower Colliery[58] on the other side of the Rhigos Mountain but certainly the last burst of communal living around the collieries, the camaraderie, the hardships, the dirt and, oh yes, the seemingly endless coal.

Treherbert and its valley head companion villages sit around the ready limits of the accessible coal measures the rapacious mine owners came to plunder. This is almost as far as you can go from the port, from the city, from the present-day work-filled Newport, Cardiff and Barry conurbation 25 miles to the south. There were once at least six large pits here

and the many spoil heaps were worth beholding. But like everywhere else in the 2020s coalfield – mostly gone, closed, wreckage of works removed, tips washed and landscaped, blackness banished. Sylvan wonder returned. Unless you look closely, of course.

There was a splendid pre-crash early new millennium proposal of architect Jonathan Adams to redevelop the blind valleys here by removing what's left of the coal tip and creating a leisure canal and tourist lake at valley top. This would be enhanced by the provision of new housing stock, a futuristic valley-side hugging hotel and an array of support enterprises. It might still happen but as the decades roll its prospect looks more and more distant[59].

We turn our back on the town and cross the tracks, the top of them, just before the final buffers, to head up, along the valley sides, to view the pit

head of the Bute Merthyr Colliery. All that remains now to mark the pit head is a low grass mound. The Bute colliery opened in 1851 and was the first steam coal pit in the Rhondda. It worked in conjunction with Lady Margaret Colliery, a short distance south of Treherbert station. There's nothing there now, either. The combined operation employed more than 800 men and closed in 1926.

We walk on, up valley, following the river, terrace backs glimpsed easily through the trees. The site of the Ty-draw Colliery sitting at the junction of the Pen Pych and Blaen Rhondda tributaries with the main Rhondda River is about as celebrated as the rest of the shafts here. Tydraw, known then as the Dunraven, was sunk in 1865 and, employing another 800, stayed the course until the Coal Board closed it in 1959.

We are at valley fork now. Ahead is Blaen Rhondda and the once enormous Fernhill Colliery. We bear west into Blaen Cwm, end of the world. It was developed to provide workers' housing for the miners at Glenrhondda Colliery when that was sunk in 1911[60]. That colliery today is as lost and uncelebrated as the rest. Ron Berry, novelist, described by fellow fictioneer Alun Richards as "the Rhondda prose gangster" and one of Wales' greatest authors lived here on Michael's Road. He describes walking the five miles south into bustling shop-filled Treorchy as an adventure. Rhondda top was an enclosed and minimalist world.

Berry wrote six novels, a sheaf of short stories and a late autobiography. When I discovered his writing – the sparkling wonder of his writing – it was late in my career. I knew his short fiction from decades back, thought I did, but from the magical Welsh steam that rose from his Valleys fiction it was clear I didn't. Here was a man with reach and depth who could encapsulate his fast evaporating subject in a few sentences. The coal seams and their winning and the effect this had on the men with the backs and brawn – their past, their stumbling, passionate present and, pretty much always, never their future. There wasn't one. There wouldn't be one. There never was one. Despite the endless class battle and the facing-off of toil against money and money always winning.

When Jack Kerouac sat on top of his forest fire look-out pole and won satori I felt similar lights coming on. When I followed John Updike's Rabbit-running before heart attack along that forgotten beach. When the children die in Hardy's Jude but the world goes on. When Joyce sparks off on his list of heroes in *Ulysses*. When Ron Berry watches the pits finally close and that world come crashing down.

Ron Berry[61] was a miner who'd worked as a boxer, a soccer player for Swansea Town, attended Coleg Harlech, fought in the Second World War and had ended as one of the most gifted, underrated, and irascibly cantankerous writers south Wales has ever produced. Wynn Thomas described him as "a prickly genius who jealously guarded the aggressive contrariness that energised his edgy talent." He was certainly one of the most difficult writers I had to deal with in my days as a literary magazine editor. But his books are superb. Set for the large part in the 1960s *Flame and Slag* in particular records, as Meic Stephens suggests, "what remains of the past before it sputters out as garbled memory". In the book Blaen Cwm stars as Darren, a fictional town, but clearly this one. He catches the real Rhondda, that sometimes happier place not regularly employed in the industrial novels of others.

Berry's house at the far end of Michael's Road has both a butterfly and a celebratory slate plaque. 'Ron Berry Writer. 1920-1997. We Abide We Hold Our Ground.' That's a quotation from his autobiography, *History Is What You Live* published in 1998. Streets here end in rising mountain. There's nowhere else to go. A path leads west for a short distance to the now blocked mouth of the 1870 Rhondda Tunnel that took that famous railway through to the Swansea

Valleys beyond. The tunnel was closed on safety grounds in 1970. Local mining had progressively distorted its structure and despite the installation of more than 500 steel ribs deterioration continued. There's an active campaign to reopen this more than three thousand metre long passageway as a pedestrian walkway and cycle track.

Our route returns through the town, a place where little moves. The active, however, may wish to take a diversion and bear north to follow the long slow zig zag right up the sides of Pen Pych, passing waterfalls, rock falls and glades to eventually access its flat top, as good as Cape Town's Table Mountain any day, and with views down valley that encapsulate everything this book has been about. Take half a day and do this.

We cross the Nant Selsig as the Rhondda River now is. It is joined by Nant y Gwair a few hundred metres further east to take on the name that made it famous. Heading east along Blaen y Cwm Road we skirt Blaen Rhondda to turn south into Tynewydd, the township that connects valley heads with the, by comparison only, vast conurbation that is Treherbert. The ghost memories of further pits dot the landscape. Tynewydd, Aber Rhondda, Fernhill. Spaces where they might have been. Tips landscaped, often imperfectly, the arms of functionless worker's terraces bending around their shapes.

The roads of Tynewydd are being resurfaced as we pass. The only activity viewable for miles, bar a man in his dressing gown smoking in his doorway and a women with a dog moving slowly across a rough stretch of grass. The fifties style block-shaped Tynewydd Labour Club and Institute at the top of Margaret Street, once home to everything from wrestling to Carols by Candlelight, is shuttered. In the one shop we find open on Wyndham Street knitting wool jostles for sale with tinned soup, bread, milk, biscuits and dry cleaning. "Trade's not like it used to be," the owner tells us.

Treherbert, traditional shop in Tynewydd

We move on from Tynewydd into Treherbert itself and, as ever, it's hard to see where the one town ends and the next begins. The Wyndham is one marker, a pub offering not only the expected 'Live Music' and 'Fine Ale' but 'Good Song', 'Cards' and 'Story Telling' too. Treherbert, the town itself, doesn't rise that much up the valley's sides, there is enough semi flat land for level streets. The valley sides themselves rise anyway, towering up in restored glory, no black stains, no tramways, nor smokestacks, nor cableways of moving buckets, birds in their air, smoke and rattle gone.

Treherbert stretches in a line south following the lowland and the Rhondda River. For the most part the streets are wide and full of light and often full of rain as more falls here than any other Valley location. Not today for us however.

The town is painter Charles Burton territory. He was born here and lived on Bute Street, famously painted many times. Burton's canvases of the sloping streets, the coal trains, the spoil tips, the view from number 72 from where he gazed, the view on up valley into Blaen Cwm are some of the best valley paintings we have. Burton caught the train daily down to Cardiff where he attended art school in The Friary. As the more than hour long daily journey unwound steadily clanking down valley he was joined on board by members of what was to become known as the Rhondda group. Tom Hughes, Robert Thomas, and Nigel Flower and then later by Gwyn Evans at Tonypandy and Ernest Zobole at Ystrad, fellow artists who filled the carriage with art discussion, fixing the creative world, sorting the future.

Burton's paintings of that place where the Rhondda runs out at the end of Michael's Road in Blaen Cwm, houses reduced to white-ended geometric shapes, telegraph poles framing the vertical view, Pen Pych shown treeless at street's end, rising into a Burton grey, make time stand. Here the Valley is seen from the inside rather than through the eyes of an impressionable visitor. How the Rhondda was, how it still is.

The grid pattern to the grey terraced streets now becomes clearly visible. On the corner of the square we pass The Bute. This is a solid Pennant stone pub that's been here as long as the town has. This being the Valleys, and rather like the ones at Porth and at Tonypandy, the square is not actually a square at all, more a wide junction. We cross to climb Church Street that would have led to St Mary's Church (1868) except that was demolished as structurally unsafe in 1967. Intrepid walkers could continue along the lane that pitches up onto the frankly dangerous Rhigos Road to return to the town passing the cleared site of the demolished Treherbert Hospital. This imposing structure lasted from 1927 until 1999. The gateposts are all that remain, iron framed and with shrub growing right up their centre. The less dramatic but clearly safer route is to return along Stuart Street to meet Bute Street just along from the fried fish enterprise of Good Pie Mr Chips and head north west from there.

Treherbert, Bute Street, 'Good Pie Mr. Chips'

Having visited the Bute Street highlights of Charles Burton's house at number 72 and the site of the Gaiety Cinema, now a branch of Spar, we head back down Station Street. In its day Station Street had grocers, cobblers, bookshops, pubs, cafés, and a great variety hall seating thousands. This was known as the Opera House. Here locals enjoyed plays, vaudeville shows, travelling circuses, films, concerts from Valley choirs and boxing matches. All ended in 1934 when, as keeps happening in these valleys, the building burned to the ground.

The road crosses the river near the 1911 Ninian Stuart Conservative Club, shuttered and dark. Ninian Stuart was the Second Marquess' son, the same Ninian as the Cardiff football ground and Roath Park highway. His statue in World War One uniform stands on a plinth in front of the National Museum. The clock-towered, columned, double-fronted, oversize and currently empty Treherbert edifice is seeking a new purpose. The actual Conservative Club, adding the word 'Unionist' to its title and retaining the 'Ninian Stuart', has moved to smaller premises round the corner.

The station stands just beyond the corrugated hanger-like structure that houses the Treherbert Boys Club. Everywhere we've seen signs of a great and active past that Treherbert has not quite got over. Old photos depict grand buildings that have out served their purpose and have often been pulled down as too expensive to keep. Many of those that do remain, like the houses which surround them, are in a poor state of repair. We need a plan. But this top of the Valleys town of the Rhondda hasn't got one yet.

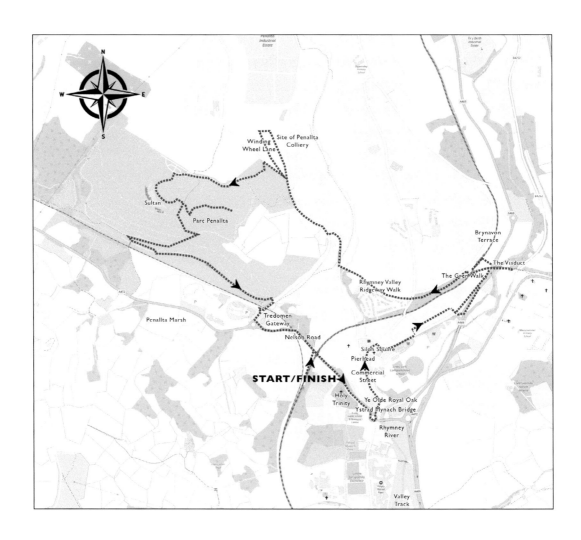

YSTRAD MYNACH

6.86 miles
www.plotaroute.com/route/1653455

This is Nelson Road, the A472, which runs alongside Nant Caeach, one of the town's three watercourses. We track it south down to its confluence with the Rhymney River. We pass Holy Trinity, architect John Norton's Lancet-style 1850s church in snecked Pennant sandstone. On its raised ground it looks the epitome of tradition. Snecked. It's a great northern English word. It means latched, which is what you do to a door, although in architecture it refers more to the way the walls are built of differing sized stones.

Beyond the church is Ystrad Mynach bridge which crosses the Rhymney near where the town's second nant, the Cylla, also joins the flow. The bridge here was one of the reasons for the town's original founding. Bridges, fords, crossings. At such places you built your hut. Today a roundabout controls incoming traffic and is faced down by the Tudor-styled Ye Olde Royal Oak. Despite aspirations to be much older this impressive drinking tavern was actually built just before World War One. Its much smaller and far less flamboyant predecessor stood on the same site for a century and a half before that.

Out on the roundabout the Council has constructed a fenced bed of grass and weeds in the shape of a giant oak leaf. It's only visible as such, however, from above, a task that's hard to manage unless you work in streetlamp maintenance or are a roofer. An interpretation board half hidden in roadside foliage offers a few paragraphs of vaguely justifiable historical interpretation. These concern the battle of Worcester of 1651 and King Charles I hiding from the Roundheads in a nearby tree. An oak naturally. History bends at our will. Flavio Biondo's fifteenth century insistence that we follow the evidence ignored again in favour of making it all sound good. Say he was here. In that tree. He possibly was. And the roundabout looks great.

Ystrad Mynach. The meaning of the town's name is lost although ask about and a lot of people claim to still know. An Ystrad is a flat valley floor like the one here where the Rhymney, Taff, Sirhowy and Ebbw all contribute. Just here Glamorgan and Monmouth once met and before them Senghenydd's medieval Is Caiach and Uwch Caiach joined hands.

Working out how Mynach, *monk*, fits the location is much harder. Colourful tales of brothers rescuing damsels, fighting Welsh princes, and killing Normans abound. No records exist of a local monastery however. Such fictions are best left unprobed or their magic will go.

South of here beyond the hospital and the college is the Valley Track. This is the only extant greyhound racing stadium left in the entire valley sweep and celebrated as a great working-class asset in the Council's 2019 Ystrad Mynach Masterplan. In this hundred page document Caerphilly Council see Ystrad Mynach as a hub. In fact they are so keen on the term that they use it forty-two times. The term is often prefaced with the words 'thriving' or 'strategic'. Ystrad Mynach, of course, is just that. A thriving hub. One of the few places in these corrugated hills where east-west traverse is just as possible as the expected north-south.

The Pierhead

Valley planners have an enthusiasm for this. The development of such a centre will free up City Region funding for an increasing number of enterprise zones, sports clusters, visitor destinations, sustainable housing builds, accessible for all improvement schemes and thriving transport hubs. Ystrad Mynach's metropolitan future will be an electric dream as the urban surge heads north building on every scrap of ground in sight.

We follow Commercial Street which bends north passing the Mini Miners Club, "for all children aged 6 weeks to 13 years", up into town. Here bright Penallta and Bedwlwyn Roads are filled with unshuttered shops: estate agents, grocers, card stores, restaurants, vape supplies, opticians, beauty parlours.

The weekend crowds are thin although there is a scattering of faces. From the front yard of the Non-Political Club, the porch of the barbers, the corner of Siloh Square, everywhere, they stand and smoke and watch us pass with our cameras round our necks.

Barbers shops, of which there are a number, are clearly the new male community centres. All are full of blokes in sweats having their faces fixed, their hair strimmed and coloured, their necks smoothed and, in a few cases, with a set of cotton buds stuck up their noses, having their nostrils cleared. Some hold babies in their arms. Others seem to have shopping on the floor beside them. What it takes to be macho in the Valleys on a Saturday morning has clearly changed.

The Jones Arcade of 1912, cuts the prow off the Pierhead, the town dominating public artwork embellished Valley flatiron building. It might not be quite up to the standard of the one at Bargoed but it's still impressive. The arcade could house a dozen stores at full throttle but has fewer today. Veg of Evans catches the eye. I buy a bag of apples.

The Pierhead originally housed the Ystrad Mynach branch of the Treharris Workingmen's Co-operative Society. That's been replaced today by the St David's Hospice Care charity shop and Mr Barbers, the only hairdresser I've come across with an advertised alcohol licence. To their front are artist Steve Joyce's blue-painted railings. He's called these *Contents* and embellished them with just that – bananas, a row of potatoes, fish heads, an engineer's pully wheel, a giant pair of scissors – all items found during the redevelopment of the stores behind. The impact is compromised slightly by the addition of Covid-distancing banners, massed busy lizzies in hanging baskets and a deal of show-through rust.

Around the corner in Siloh Square Yorkshire sculptor Rachel Fenner's ensemble of Celtic font, engraved benches, tessellated spirals and mosaic half dome has been comprehensively amended by the council. In 2014 faced with serial vandalism and becoming increasingly unsafe the Council rejected the artist's £700 repair estimate and had the offending items removed and the detail flattened. What's left almost a decade on might be safe but it's hardly art.

As a centre of the literary universe Ystrad Mynach fares badly. As far as I can tell there are no local bards of distinction nor is YM the setting for any classic Anglo-Welsh industrial novels. Tripp didn't come here to read and cause mayhem at the pub. The Ystrad Mynach Poetry Festival hasn't happened yet. Inspirational verse sourced from school workshops and then spread about the town in inventive and usually illegible ways doesn't feature anywhere until we get to Penallta. You are safe with verse. Almost everyone not practising the art doesn't understand it at all.

HENGOED

Sun drenched and for once enjoying the ability to see distant horizons we walk on towards Hengoed. Pretty much Ystrad Mynach according to the Council's Masterplan (along with Nelson, Penallta, Gelligaer, Penpedairheol, Cascade, and Tiryberth). These are distinct townships for those who live here but all Ystrad Mynach when viewed from above. Avoiding the traffic on the A469 we track instead The Avenue, a roll of Hyacinth Bucket bungalows with not a tree in sight.

Ahead is one of the two things that Hengoed is famous for. The viaduct. A splendid sixteen arch piece of Thomas Kennard's Victorian railway engineering. It was built in 1858 to carry the Newport, Abergavenny and Hereford railway that linked Neath with Pontypool. For a century it served Hengoed and nearby Maesycwmmer offering an alternative to the Rhymney Rail line from Rhymney to Cardiff Queen Street.

The viaduct was closed in the Beeching cuts in 1964 and the tracks lifted. In 2005 it was reopened as a walking route and as part of Sustrans' National Cycle Route 47 which runs from Newport to Fishguard. Access from where we are involves passing the open Junction Inn (Rock + Roll on Saturday, Rugby on Sunday, Chinese curry, rice, spring roll and a pint £10) and on over Hengoed station itself.

Hengoed's second claim to fame is as the birthplace near the viaduct of the cartoonist Gren. A walking trail in his honour complete with Gren embellished benches crosses the valley here. Gren was Grenfell Jones who died in 2007. His cartoons, including the weekly strip *Ponty and Pop* in the *Western Mail*, entered south Wales culture. He designed album sleeves for Max Boyce, created the village of Aberflyarff, majored on sheep with slogans on their sides and drawings of valley streets looping impossibly along valley sides.

The Gren Walk, a gentle couple of miles running north from the viaduct to Flower (Fleur-de-lis) and back takes in Gren's birthplace on Brynavon Terrace along with places and sights typical of those appearing in his cartoons.

A diversion to cross the viaduct to the Maesycwmmer side offers unrivalled views up and down valley. On the eastern viaduct side stands the *Stargate*, the local name for Andy Hazell's 2010 *Wheel O Drams*, a 8.5 metre ring of painted galvanised steel coal wagons complete with company logos, minor graffiti and no damage yet. Public art in these townships is consistent in its presence and the fact that almost always it is created by someone from elsewhere. Much like the railways and the collieries the art often celebrates. Nothing new under the valley sun.

Wheel o Drams by Andy Hazell

Our route on, heading west now, takes the Taff Vale extension to the Rhymney Valley Ridgeway Walk. We follow what were once Great Western railtracks to emerge from the trees at the lower end of the Penallta Link Road. Pen alltau – top of the wooded slopes. Uphill for a while.

PENALLTA

Penallta Colliery comes into view ahead on Winding Wheel Lane. Both sets of headgear remain in place next to the brick and window-faced bulk of the powerhouse. Penallta was a late sinking (1905) and became the super-pit jewel of the Powell Duffryn empire. This was the pit chosen for extension, mechanisation, modernisation and facilities investment every time rationalisation in the mining industry came to the boil. And as the twentieth century rolled it came to the boil often.

Penallta was a show pit. If foreign visitors needed a demonstration of how British industry was a world beater then it was to Penallta they were taken. The pit was the deepest and largest in the coalfield and at its peak the employer of 3208 men. It was owned by the largest coalfield operator in the UK with more than 70 collieries in south Wales alone.

It was one of the first to benefit from recently developed power loaders which meant fully mechanised coal faces. When slumps came it was always Penallta that survived. The pit was even maintained beyond the eighties miners strike. Penallta became the Tory government's industrial face of the future. It had hi-tech skip winding, automated coal washing and computerised coal crushing.

But nothing lasts and nor ultimately did Penallta. Despite the continuing need for coal at Aberthaw and at Port Talbot steelworks, two big Penallta customers, operations were closed as uneconomic in 1991. A photograph I've seen taken from above on one of the last days of working shows a highly ordered scene with repairs in place and wreckage banished. The pit baths, from the roof of which the shot was taken, were in perfect shape. The last shift came up from this deepest of mines and marched out with a brass band playing at their head.

When they opened in 1938 those baths were hailed as a modern pit miracle. They had more than 4000 lockers and 250 shower cubicles. The building was constructed in the then revolutionary international modern style, all flat slab

roofs and white-edged Bauhaus windows. This was in stark contrast to the Edwardian factory look of the rest of the enormous pit. CADW were quick to grade list both this building ('one of the finest examples of this building type to survive in the United Kingdom') and the remainder of the surface structures (although the giant washery with its huge concrete funnel appears to have gone). Just what benefits that listing brought are moot. The buildings can't be demolished nor can they be converted without approval. But they can certainly be allowed to simply dissolve and fade.

The pit head baths, approached through thickets of buddleia and protected by metal mesh fencing, are clad in ivy, have trees growing from their flat roofs and appear on the edge of collapse. The lamp room and the great engineering building have already been saved, enveloped, and converted into multiple-occupancy flats (£120K a time according to the estate agent's window in town). More conversions are in the planning stages with the great powerhouse the next target and thirty-three apartments due to be made from the wreck of the bathhouse. 'Live/Work opportunities' the brochure advertises. But progress is slow. Beyond the new Cwm Calon housing estate encroaches slowly uphill across former mine surface territory.

Beyond Penallta the Pit lies Penallta the Parc. Its entrance is opposite the bath house and is most effectively strewn with public artwork made to resemble the kind of industrial detritus typically found at the heads of pits. This is the work of blacksmith Andrew Rowe who has created great rusted

Corten steel panels and made them resemble, he says, the scattered pages of a notebook.

With some earth shifting and much tree planting the Parc is a reclamation of what was once one of the biggest coal tips in Europe. This was a black disturbance in the continuum rivalled in south Wales only by the champion that was at Bargoed and the killing fields of Ffos-y-Fran opencast at Dowlais. Like the deserts of Arabia or the burning forests of Amazon these things are visible from space.

The work converting Parc Penallta has been a great success. Mick Petts' great slice of land art in the form of *Sultan the Pony* dominates park centre. The park's events arena needed sheltering from the prevailing winds. Rather than simply having a 60,000 ton bank of coal shale doing the job the Parc developers employed land artist Petts to create a sculptural form that had relevance to the location. The last pony working underground got his release. He's visible on OS maps as a contour line, a cartoon drawing of a galloping animal on an otherwise sombre map face. You can walk across his back, tread where his hoofs do and only see him as anything like a pony from half way up the nearby hill.

The arena here, a great flat expanse, has seen a couple of annual music festivals (almost always featuring Seasick Steve), extreme sports for all the family (rock climbing, skateboarding and sky diving – take your pick), Earthhour lights-off view the stars evenings, mass lantern parading, storytelling, and the annual several day Ystrad Mynach festival rival to Glastonbury – Glastonselfy[62].

In the distance looking south are the omnipresent still-extant tips of Llanbradach. From this viewpoint the distinctive poured black salt look is modified but their presence as valley tips remains.

We climb up to the highest point in the park, an eminence that looks back over Ystrad Mynach and Hengoed and on up the Rhymney Valley beyond. Here stands Malcolm Robertson's *High Point Observatory*, a giant two-storey steel crown, its struts engraved with faces, animals, miner's lamps, pitheads and houses. The path below zig zags down through a thick treescape towards the Nant Caeach. John, with uncharacteristic adventure, suggests a deviation from the stone surfaced wide pathway to take a steep and sliding zig almost vertically through the trees.

Most walks benefit from some sort of adventure. Getting lost is the standard and which is what I imagine we now are, phone signal vanished so I can't check, and nothing visible but trees which prevents any idea I might have of using a compass. But the path drops us neatly almost at valley bottom. We are now on the metalled surface of the twenty-seven mile Rhymney Valley Ridgeway Walk which connects the Sirhowy Valley Country Park with the Taff Trail. To the west is Nelson. But we head east, back towards Ystrad Mynach.

The path skirts Penallta Marsh which could provide a neat diversion hunting for the advertised on the interpretation board purple hairstreak butterflies or even for trainspotting. Through the trees John's ear picks out a revving class 37 diesel hauling coal along the freight-only line from Dowlais. Coal, still moving in these valleys but not for much longer. Climate change is seeing to that. Its source, Ffos-y-Fran, is due to close in a year or two.

Parc Penallta – Malcom Robertson's
High Point Observatory

TREDOMEN AND BACK

The Parc pathway now turns almost unremarked into the Hengoed Taff Vale Extension which offers traffic-free communing with the natural world almost right back to Ystrad Mynach station. But keen to see how the real world is managing we take the road route. This follows the edge of Tredomen Business Park passing the Dan Dare architecture of Tredomen Gateway, home to a bunch of Caerphilly education support services.

Before it was cleaned up and turned into a soft hands technology park Tredomen was the site of Powell Duffryn's headquarters and their engineering works where just about anything needed for pit work was manufactured. This ranged from axes to coal drams and everything in between. Operations continued post nationalisation with the creation on this site of the National Coal Board's Engineering Works and the location of their first computer. Back then computers could not be incorporated into the back of your watch – they filled rooms.

At the train station again we fervently wish that Nancy's Transport Café had survived. In the front garden of Station House (1858) a fierce looking dog and a dozing tabby cat lie next to each other in the sun. On the news last night Lauren Price local Olympic gold winning boxer was being welcomed home. "It's an achievement for the whole village" remarked one interviewee. It's that for sure. Train next back to the city.

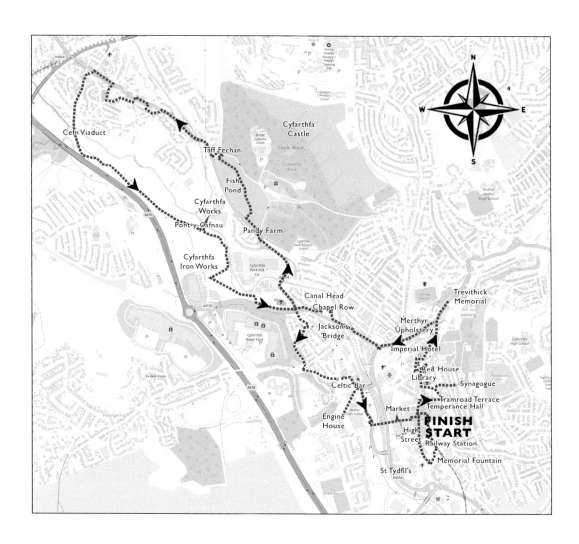

MERTHYR TYDFIL

5.88 miles
www.plotaroute.com/route/1748022

Back when it counted reaching Merthyr was like reaching Gomorrah, a place of roaring immorality, streaking sparks and gouts of fire. There were 305 pubs in Merthyr in 1850. In Cardiff in the same period there were 93. Gambling, prostitution, theft, bare knuckle fighting and drunken brawls were endemic. The townscape seethed and suppurated with endless dust and smoke. Its houses leant against each other and when they didn't they fell down. Sanitation was non-existent. Infant death was at 50%. The population grew daily.

In the mid eighteenth century Merthyr was a village of around forty thatched houses with a population of a few hundred, a Welsh place of ancient Welsh martyrdom. Saint Tydfil, the twenty-third daughter of Brychan, King of Brycheiniog was murdered here in 480. Her remains are dust somewhere beneath the church dedicated to her in the centre of the town. Following the discovery of new processes of iron making and the establishment of the first large-scale Merthyr ironworks the town's population began to rise. By 1801 it was 7705. By 1851 it was 46,378. Merthyr was now the largest town in Wales.

What drew the Welsh and the Irish to this iron town at the heads of the Valleys, at the edge of the moors, where the winds blew and natural shelter was scarce was money. You could earn it here like you could nowhere else in Wales. The new iron masters were creating new wealth. A brand new proletariat was providing it.

Barges from the bustling port of Cardiff would come up twenty-five miles and fifty locks taking a good three days to reach this outpost. Brunel brought the trains in 1841, building a standard gauge track that cut the journey time from days to hours. This delivered even more wealth to the ironmasters and by now coal exploiters at valley top, here in Merthyr. The population grew again.

Merthyr, central to that belt of ironstone that runs across the south Wales valley tops, hosted four major ironworks – Cyfarthfa, Dowlais, Plymouth and Penydarren – along with a run of smaller subsidiaries. It was surrounded by coal pits and limestone quarries enabling the new English masters

Merthyr Tydfil, Robert and Lucy Thomas Memorial Fountain

of industry and exploiters of the working class to make unbelievable fortunes. This period of blossoming population, sprawling town growth and massive production lasted not much more than a century. By the time of Victoria's death iron production had turned to steel production and driven by the exigencies of economics was largely being produced elsewhere. The boom was over and when the great depression arrived was completely done.

Some production hung on into the later decades of the twentieth century but by the 1980s even coal extraction had ceased. Factories and light engineering enterprises led by Hoover, Thorne Electrical, Remploy, Standard Box, and other others were established in the vicinity to help stave off mass redundancy among the still, for a valley town, huge population. Most ultimately failed.

Unemployment returned and with it poor health and fecklessness. As Rachel Trezise describes the present day town in *Dial M For Merthyr*: "Post-industrial Merthyr, where fly-by-night factories had replaced mines and ironworks and TV and pop music had swept away chapel religion…". Rachel, one of those rare things, a female novelist writing in the Valleys, comes from Treorchy but like most valley residents knows Merthyr well.

Merthyr's reputation flies ahead of it. It is the most written about town in Wales declares Joe England[63]. Not only does Merthyr act as a magnet for historians the country over looking for the working-class origins of the twenty-first century Welsh but it is also the setting for the whole genre of industrial fictions that form the centrepiece of the Anglo-Welsh literary tradition. Alexander Cordell's *The Fire People*, Jack Jones' *Bidden to the Feast*, Gwyn Thomas' *All Things Betray Thee*, Geraint Lewis' *Ghosts of China*, Des Barry's *A Bloody Good Friday*, and Glyn Jones' *The Island of Apples*. These are stories of the teeming life that went on here. They are full of fire and fortune, revolution and war, love, strikes, lockouts and the endless struggle of the worker against the owner and the clashing of the forces that both sides found themselves able to muster.

Nineteenth and early twentieth century life in Merthyr was tough. In the twenty-first things are better but inevitably issues remain. Life expectancy here is among the lowest in Wales while poor diet and obesity rates are among the highest. Rates for alcohol misuse register as the worst for anywhere in Wales, and by a considerable margin. With these stats in mind I expect to see alcoholics on the benches and bulbous obesity in the supermarkets but there's no more of that than there is anywhere else. By contrast Merthyr is bright, people-filled, and among Valley towns bustlingly normal.

TOWN

Arriving at the main station, the only station come to that, we are greeted by an illuminated sign telling us that the train we've just travelled up on has been cancelled. The conductor waves his hands in the air. Mike Jenkins, who greets us in the car park, is completely unfazed. "Happens all the time." Mike, a poet of long standing, who lives up the hill in Merthyr's Heolgerrig has agreed to accompany us for the first part of the walk.

The station we've reached is a shadow of a shadow of its former self. A single track hitting a single set of buffers. Passengers emerge to find themselves in the centre of a giant Tesco car park. The Tesco store itself has been built where the High Street station stood from 1851 to 1962. This was an impressive Brunel-designed replica of the Great Western's glass and soaring iron structure at Paddington. Rail stations once marked a place. Merthyr in the last century was important enough to have two: the present one at High Street, a meeting place for the rail tracks of five companies; and the Taff Vale station at Plymouth Street, a short step away.

Mike Jenkins, as we've discovered elsewhere on our Valleys' walks, is a contemporary poet producing work that appeals across a broad spectrum. He has lived here since 1980 and writes with fluidity in the local dialect. It's won him a whole raft of admirers.

Personlee I carn wait
f glbal blydi warmin–
'magine Costa Merthyr
an savin on-a train fare
t Barry Islan' an further.

Jest think of all-a vineyards
on-a illsides over Troedyrhiw[64]

Mike is a rare example of those who were anarchist while at college and have spent their entire lives since moving further left. His tour of central Merthyr with us is dotted with tales of rebellion and protest. This town has revolution at its heart. The Merthyr Rising of 1831, the martyrdom of Dic Penderyn, its taverns hotbeds of Chartism, Socialism and Communism. Keir Hardy, founder of the Labour Party, was Merthyr's turn of the century MP. S.O. Davies, trades union official and miner was its rebel Labour MP for most of the twentieth century. Little wonder the radical tradition hangs visibly here.

South beyond the car park with its blossom of signs announcing 'Town Centre Regeneration Station Access Improvements', already looking slightly jaded, stands the Robert and Lucy Thomas Memorial Fountain[65].

The fountain's open canopy is elaborate and extensively decorated. During one of its moves the drinking troughs were lost as was the fountain. Its purpose now impossible the canopy remains as a listed memory of what was. Coal and Iron. With a total lack of irony it was manufactured in Glasgow rather than Merthyr.

To the square's west and on the site of St Tydfil's martyrdom stands the well restored St Tydfil's Old Parish Church of 1894. The graveyard is inner-city immaculate. 'St Tydfil's Graveyard Restored Under Operation Eyesore By The Merthyr Tydfil Borough Council in 1973' reads a sign.

We leave heading north. On the corner of Salmon Street, Mike points outs the former and much protested outside UKIP offices, now doing service as The House of Beauty.

We pass Merthyr's oldest still standing pub, the Crown, with its proudly displayed date of origin – 1785. This place has been a hot bed of alternatives for centuries. Women's chartist groups met here. Dic Penderyn's supporters plotted here. In recent times its Plaid-supporting landlord allowed independence meetings, CND gatherings and performances by Mike's Red Poets. Ifor Thomas and Ian McMillan have both read here.

Around the corner on Swan Street stands a rather incongruously modern-looking small office block. In its day this was the Union House of the AEU and the place where the Marxist historian Gwyn Alf Williams honed his recollections of revolution. Here he delivered a ten lecture series that later became the source material for Gwyn's best-selling history book and TV series, made with his political polar-opposite Wynford Vaughan Thomas, *The Dragon Has Two Tongues*.

Up High Street, a refreshingly non-boarded and pretty lively thoroughfare, we encounter the first of the dozen or so poetry benches. Each contains a quote from a local writer. Mike's is from his first book *The Common Land*. John photographs the poet pointing the words out. Next door is Idris Davies. Further on appear Harri Webb, Grahame Davies, Glyn Jones, Alexander Cordell, the entire lyrics to Joseph Parry's 'Myfanwy' and this: "Merthyr at night is beautiful, the sky is illuminated with deep red glow…while the furnaces breathe forth their volumes of fire", quoted, the bench says, from Joseph Onwhyn's *Welsh Tourist Guide* of 1840 proving that local authorities, and especially it seems this one (see St Tydfil's Church), can be wittily informal when they want to be.

We take a right to briefly divert up John Street to view the Temperance Hall. This is currently being turned into a bar and club. The structure originates from 1852 when it was a centre of abstinence. It was rebuilt in 1888 as the 1350-seat Scala Cinema and then in 1985 turned into a snooker club with bar (which also mounted events including appearances by Attila the Stockbroker and Barnstormer). After that it was dereliction although no fire which is often the fate of such structures. Check when you pass. By this time I'm sure the serving of alcohol will be back.

We cross to the end of Tramroad Terrace where the shell of the Miner's Hall crumbles under the weight of buddleia and bramble. Grade II listed, deserted since its existence as Charbonnier's Nightclub ended in fire in 1992, the place is currently ownerless. The building began life in 1855 as the Brunel-designed Siloh Chapel. It was turned into the Miner's Hall in 1921. By 1987 it was doing time selling beer at night and offering glittering dances. Turning what's left into flats or new houses appears to be beyond the powers.

Top of rising Church Street on Bryntirion Road stands the double-turreted former Merthyr Synagogue of 1877. It's been empty since 2006 and there are plans to convert it to a Jewish Heritage Centre. Round the back someone has daubed the words 'Thou Shalt Not….' across a door lest an interloper might determine to trespass seeking shelter.

We are in Penderyn Square, outside the Red House now. Ty Coch. "No one calls it that," Mike tells me. Epicentre of the rising. The place where in 1900 Keir Hardy made revolutionary speeches from the balcony. Where Mike has read to 5000 Yes Cymru supporters and where I, long ago, stood at 9.30 one dull morning reading sound poems to the walkers about to set out on Made in Roath's *Red March* back to Cardiff.

The festering of discontent among the working class came to a head here in 1831. Wages were being lowered. Men were being laid off. The whole area rose. In June of that year 10,000 protestors marched on the magistrates and iron masters holed up in the Castle Inn. The red flag was carried. There were shouts of 'Caws a bara' (cheese and bread) and 'I lawr â'r Brenin' (down with the king). In the drawn out days of battle parts of the town were sacked, the debtor's court wrecked and in the riots premises were looted and soldiers were stabbed. Twenty-four protestors were killed.

Among those protestors eventually arrested, two – Lewis Lewis (Lewsyn yr Heliwr) and Richard Lewis (Dic Penderyn) were sentenced to death. Lewis Lewis had his sentence commuted to transportation. Dic Penderyn was hanged at Cardiff Goal – outside Cardiff Market – in 1831.

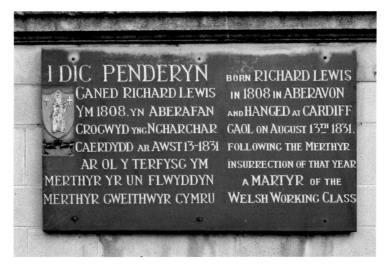

He was innocent. Attempts down the long decades to formally pardon Penderyn have all failed. Despite the current culture for state leaders and grand kahunas to be seen publicly beating their breasts in apology for the past actions of their people it is amazing that Dic Penderyn's imaginary crimes remain in place.

But the Library does bear a Dic Penderyn plaque and leaning against the wall of a shop's gable end is David Appeyard's Iron Heart (based on a design detail on the parapet of Merthyr's famous iron bridge over the Taff). Below, across two somewhat illegible sandstone slabs, is a commissioned poem from Gillian Clarke.

> They gathered beneath the peaks of Pen-y-Fan,
> Corn Ddu, Cribyn, and soldiers shot them down.
> Lament injustice, slaughter, the good man
> hanged as a warning: Dic Penderyn.

There'll also be a plaque to the sixty killed in the Rising installed in the new bus station. Mike has been agitating.

Next door to the Red House is Merthyr's Portland stone Arts and Crafts style Carnegie Library. Out front on a plinth is a statue of one of Merthyr's empire-period great and good. This one is a berobed Henry Seymour Berry (d. 1928) done in bronze by Goscombe John. The front plaque tells us that. On one side, however, in full Pharaonic style the statue gets renamed as William Ewart Berry (d. 1954) and on the other as James Gomer Berry (d. 1968). Press barons all. One of Dic might have been better.

At the square's edge we run into the figurative artist Gus Payne[66] whose paintings offer a rich mix of mythology, folklore, hoody culture and other contemporary symbols. His striking work is as alarming as it is satisfying. It was he, working as arts officer for the local council, who steered the authority into funding the poetry benches we saw earlier.

High Street rolls. We stop for tea at Soar, the refurbished Welsh-medium chapel now an active café, shop and Welsh-medium community centre. The language's re-penetration of the Valleys is at its lowest in Merthyr. Surprising given the area's early immigration of workers from rural Wales. But I am assured that things are improving.

Pre-covid the Imp, The Imperial Hotel just further up High Street, was a centre for many of Mike's poetry and revolutionary ventures. Paul Groves came to read bringing his own giant lectern. The Belgian-Irish poet Anne Cluysenaar came with a clock so she wouldn't overrun and then did. She left the clock at the pub. There were countless others. Poetry hangs in its air. The pub has been refurbished and relaunched now as The Tiger Inn[67] reusing the name it was born with at the start of the nineteenth century. The change to The Imperial happened during a refurbishment in 1861.

Will the readings return as Covid fades? "Probably not, too posh."

High Street now crosses the culverted Morlais Brook and runs into Penydarren Road. The brook is a central feature of Glyn Jones' fine Merthyr schooldays novel *The Island of Apples*. In the book Jones lives with his family at Dragon Mills, a clothing maker at the turn of the nineteenth century. Jones' inspiration, the three story stone-built premises of Merthyr Upholstery, still exists. As does the brook which the premises faces. The building has been bought by electrical contractor Ross Perriman who is planning on converting to an Air B&B. Try staying there, you'll sleep in a piece of literary history.

A hundred metres up on the right stands the Trevithick Memorial. Next door was the grand 1800 seat Theatre Royal and Opera House, now a shell. The memorial was installed before a crowd of 3000 in 1934 on the centenary of the engineer's death. Hard to imagine that many fans turning out today. It consists of a quarter scale replica of Trevithick's engine built from melted tramrails and standing atop a plinth built from chair stones recovered from the Penydarren tramroad itself.

Why here? The entrance to the Penydarren ironworks where the engine was constructed were just up the road and the tramway tracks began at this spot. John is busy photographing a trio of passing women who have agreed to pose below the memorial. The three graces. Such diversions are common on our walks.

High Street now done, the atmosphere shifts. Opposite stand a run of frontages, deserted and derelict. The graffitied red and yellow brick of the boarded-up YMCA[68], the damp pocked pillars of the 1810 Masonic Temple, the war memorial, and the dole office, freakishly feeble now in its single-leaf façade. They've been wrecked for decades, changing only with the graffiti that gets sprayed to their fronts. Currently, as we pass, a bold protestor swirls a red banner while John Lennon stares hard through round sunglasses. 'Choose Plaid Cymru Choose Life'. Mike has used the banner waver for the front of his latest book, *Anonymous Bosch*[69].

Bethesda Street drops us to the top edge of what was once known as China. The first of Merthyr's three[70] statued boxers is here. Eddie Thomas was British Empire and European Welterweight Champion. 'Bachgen bach ô Colliers Row', a little boy from Collier's Row. He went on to become a conservative Mayor, Freeman and Councillor of this deeply left-leaning borough. This might account for why he's here, out on the green edge of town, space and air around him. His people's champion fellows have their plinths in the centre of bustling town.

Charismatic minister Methusalem Jones' Bethesda chapel was here, one of Merthyr's earliest, Welsh faith shared with Soar back on High Street. Deconsecrated in 1976 the building ran as an arts centre for a few years until that, too, failed and Merthyr let it go. All that remains is a plaque and mosaic replica set back among bushes.

We part with Mike, walking on north. Still Merthyr. John and I cross the river on the new A4102 that touches the southern edge of the land on which were built the Cyfarthfa Works.

If you get the job of naming a town's districts then 'China' is not an obvious choice. It's one, though, that Merthyr somehow got saddled with. No-one today is quite sure how this knot of inner-city lawlessness acquired the name of a whole country. Might be that the place was a forbidden city, full of immigrant dope dealers, prostitutes, thieves and chancers. 'China' was the only unofficial appellation to appear regularly in the police courts reports in the early 1800s newspapers. Ordnance Survey adopted it. It's there on the first maps bounded by the canal and the Abermorlais tip. You entered through an arch at the top of Dixon Street. The houses fell in to each other. Floors were mud. There was no running water. Disease rife. But life vibrant.

That was then. Napoleonic-era Merthyr at the dawn of the industrial age. The area has gone through a few generations of rebuilds since those days and apart from the Victorian terrace of Dixon Street consists entirely of ugly 80s brick offices housing the Job Centre and various branches of Merthyr's Social Services. Council recycling bags visible at the roadsides. No pubs. Nowhere to gather.

Rather than following the once tramroad-carrying Jackson's Bridge over the river we take the Swansea Road. This briefly tracks the line of the Glamorgan Canal, at the time a cutting edge enterprise. Cutting edges in the early 1800s were slow and often gentle things.

The canal and its towpath have been lost to time although a small section, without water, has been excavated at Chapel Row to front a short stub of terraced houses. One of them, the birthplace of Joseph Parry, the composer of 'Myfanwy'[71], has been turned into a Saint Fagans style living history museum. Naturally, as we are out of season today, the door is locked, as, I'm reliably told, it is most of the time. A sense of Victorian Merthyr life can be glimpsed through the windows. Sparsely furnished, hard surfaces, a bed pressed against the window's edge.

Parry was born in 1841. During his childhood he would have looked out not only onto the canal but at the bottom end of Crawshay's works. Timber yards. Graving docks. Clank and clamour. The Fever Hospital was on rising ground behind Chapel Row. Two cottages up was Cyfarthfa, the chapel itself. A shell in a photograph I've seen taken in 1951.

Less than that still standing today. High on the wall is a plaque to Jack Jones, the novelist, who immortalised the Joseph Parry story in his novel *Off To Philadelphia in the Morning* (1947).

The cottage has a bunch of unlabelled historic artefacts strewn across the grass yard outside. An early iron bridge brought here from Rhydycar. Canal boundary stones. Tram-plates. Pieces from a cast iron road bridge. Two tramway drams, one falling in on itself under the weight of weather and time.

A little further up was the Canal Head. A significant spot from where Crawshay's barge boat enterprise to shift his output first took form. 568 feet above sea level this was the highest reached by any canal in Wales. Water was delivered by leat from the iron works. It lasted from 1790 until subsidence mid-twentieth century below Aberfan and breaches at Cilfynydd made further use impossible. The last working section of the canal closed in 1944.

We sit at the picnic table outside the Dragon Grill next to Platinum Car Sales at the end of the Cyfarthfa Park Industrial Estate and look over the road at where Canal Head once lay. Green now. No memory at all. The bacon roll I buy is twice the size I'd get in Cardiff.

Pandy Farm with its ecclesiastical-looking low tower and iconic three-sided blue-faced clock points the way up to the Castle. From the forecourt among the cannon we look out at the place where Crawshay's Pandemonium, his vast iron works, once stood with their night sky illuminating never extinguished furnaces and their hellscape of molten metal and glowing cinder. Today, on the other side of the valley, just beyond, along the ridge that was Merthyr's brick-works, stands Cyfathrfa's twenty-first century successor in the form of Trago Mill's mile long 17-tower castellated hyper-market. It's a Mars-spaceship hangar big enough to fly planes in and which sells everything available in the entire world.

The last time I'd stood here at Cyfarthfa had been in the late 80s in the company of the novelist and poet Glyn Jones. We'd come to attend a conference on the Welsh industrial novel. As I've already suggested this was a form at which Glyn excelled although never in the style (nor with the money turning burn) of Alexander Cordell. At conferences Cordell would not answer questions unless they'd been sub-mitted to him two weeks in advance. "You don't get caught out that way," he said. "People love to catch you." By contrast Glyn would engage with anything. As Meic Stephens said of him "Glyn Jones' gift is that he has always known how to make of the blemished and unlovable an unexplainable song.[72]"

Cyfarthfa had been the triumphal masterpiece of ironmaster William Crawshay. 15 towers, 72 rooms, 365 windows, built on the cheap out of dark and rough local Pennant sandstone by Robert Lugar in 1824. In *The Buildings of Wales*, Newman says that the structure "gives close to little pleasure" although I'm not sure I agree. It leaks, it needs investment, but it soldiers on. Highlight on this visit is the museum and gallery that fill most of the former family spaces. Here is a history of Merthyr, its metal workings, its mines, its religious experiences, its paintings.

What makes this museum such a joy is the offbeat and disparate nature of the exhibits. Centrepiece in the former morning room is a case containing yet another model of Trevithick's locomotive, this one made from Meccano by Colin Davies of Potters Bar and presented to the Museum in 2011. There's a bust of Keir Hardy, a case of bronze age axe heads, and another containing family memorabilia including the programme of a performance mounted at Christmas 1867 entitled *Chrononhotonthologos*. The Crawshays were word benders ahead of their time.

I get the feeling that Cyfarthfa with its commanding views of the valley, its unassailable place in history and its extravagant rolling swards could offer so much more than it does. And the plans are there. A new Cyfarthfa Foundation led by former WNO chair Geraint Talfan Davies has recently produced a 70 point proposal that would create a Greater Cyfarthfa of high level glass walkways, soaring iron roads, rescuing what remains of the Crawshays' furnaces, and "healing the wounded landscape" by doubling the size of the grounds. These are ambitious ideas and some money has already been raised. Progress will depend on the developing of new Unique Selling Points. But we're not there yet. No Louvre Santes Tydfil, no Celtic nations capital, no Merthyr spaceport, no replica of the great pyramids where Ogham would have replaced the hieroglyph, no Las Vegas of the Valleys. None of those. But then there's a time to go and there's a good man at the top. Allegedly when he asked a well know broadcaster and expert on the great building what he'd do with Cyfarthfa the answer he got was "pull it down".

We leave walking north via the lake. Crawshay's fish pond and boating pool fed by a leat from the Taff Fechan further north again and originally feeding its waters on down to the great ironworks below. Cyfarthfa Park is completely municipal now with benches, bowling greens, bird feeding points and fishing pegs. Flocks of ducks take off and land on the lake in slowly squawking formation. A miniature railway runs in a swirl of loops on its elevated benches to the south. Silent when we pass but a squall of steam and tooting petrol hydraulic in season serviced by slightly portly men in uniform overalls, railway hats and white moustaches.

CEFN COED Y CYMMER

We cross the Taff Fechan by the new bridge (1910) which stands next to the much more picturesque old bridge (1775) into the lower reaches of Cefn Coed y Cymmer. This is another land of pubs by the look of it, but closer inspection shows most of them to be once pubs. Now closed and converted to private residences. Cefn, or Bucket Town, for its lack of piped water as the Victorians nicknamed it, hangs onto its age, cottaged streets, runs of terrace, new build absent, chapels prevalent, although the constant traffic on High Street makes it hard for the village to breathe.

The people who first lived here came to work at the limestone quarries or at Crawshay's ironworks. There was a railway station, a line to Merthyr and to Brecon, an electric tram running from the Rising Sun back to the shopping heart of big city Merthyr. Twenty pubs and the grand Station Hotel. Still extant. Addlestones beer. 'NO KIDS unless sitting quietly or having a meal' 'Mask's Welcome'. Anti-vaxers stay away.

We emerge on the smooth path which crosses the Cefn Viaduct, known locally as the arches. This wonder of the south Wales Valleys, a graceful curve of fifteen arches built in 1866 carried the rail line from Merthyr to Brecon until Beeching stopped all that in the 60s.

Half way through its original build, as a companion to the successful but smaller viaduct just upline at Pontsarn, the stone masons went on strike. The 115 feet high structure was completed in brick. Hard to discern today. The structure's curve, an iron information panel tells me, was in order to avoid Crawshay land, although I've heard this hotly disputed. The route bends south west above the fluster of the Taff Fechan. A woman out walking her dog tells me that I should

return in winter to see the icicles stalactiting down from the arches. Grade II listed the viaduct was refurbished for walkers and incorporated into the Taff Trail and Route 8 of the National Cycle Network in time for the new millennium.

The trail south, for that is what we now use, submerges itself in greenery. Traffic noise is reduced to the occasional slush, the wild world is back among the trees. That this place, the one we are now walking into, was once the greatest of industrial achievements, the largest iron works world-wide and the very making of a whole country is hard to credit. No echoes impinge, not here, no streaks of anything in the ever-green landscape.

CYFARTHFA IRON WORKS

The Crawshays who became the masters of this Welsh outpost were the ones to personally make the most out of the iron trade. They might not have established the Cyfarthfa works but they were certainly the ones who moved it from minor to major, turning the single blast furnace of 1786 into six by 1810 and eleven supplemented by eighteen balling furnaces by 1845. Production went through the roof.

Richard Crawshay, the Yorkshire iron merchant took over the fledgling Cyfarthfa from Anthony Bacon who had founded it in 1765 and passed it on to his son William Crawshay I although it was William Crawshay II, the grandson, who built the castle and established Cyfarthfa's reputation as an iron land big enough to have its own king. His son, Robert, became sole manager of the works in 1867 at a time when the enterprise employed more than 5000 people and the business had expanded to include a refitted works and a series of Crawshay-owned quarries, iron pits, and collieries to feed it.

But the world was not a permanent elevator towards ever greater success, it never is. Falling demand and a drop in prices led to strikes and worker confrontations. Mass un-employment followed and things did not go well. Robert Thompson Crawshay's grave in the churchyard at Vaynor, a few miles to the north of here, is worth visiting. His fourteen feet deep Victorian grave has been overlaid with a nine ton slab of reddish Radyr conglomerate seven foot two inches wide, eleven foot two inches long, and one foot two inches thick. Its unexpected dominating presence seems to crush the earth beneath it. Across its centre are the words "God Forgive Me".

The greenery thins and one of the very few traces of Merthyr's world beating iron trade appears on the left. This is Pont-y-Cafnau, the iron-made bridge of troughs. It was built for Cyfarthfa in 1793 to bring water and the limestone tramway from the Gurnos quarries directly into the works. Say Gurnos to most people and they'll recite a litany of drug misuse, knife violence and criminal damage but the place has a better history than that. The not very imposing bridge is early and a relic of an age that's gone from us almost without leaving a trace. Who would use iron bar as a construction material today? It's closed for repairs when we pass although there's little sign either of damage that needs fixing nor actually any fixing in process. Just the river flowing beneath.

Ahead is where the works were. Cyfarthfa's 158 acres of soul destroying, money creating and life providing iron puddling furnaces, rolling mills, forges, coke ovens, waterwheels, charging houses and casting sheds. This is the place that at night presented the world with a replica of Dante's inferno. Its roar, rolling, sluicing, and thunderous hammering never ceased. For decades at a stretch the furnaces were never extinguished. Day and night the work just went on.

Remains of furnaces at Cyfarthfa

What's left now, amazingly, is pretty much nothing. A whole slice of Wales' past, inconveniently reminding us of how we were and potentially costing a whole lot just to keep standing has been completely cleared. The land is empty again. Grass grows. Why wouldn't it.

However there is a little still standing. Six blast furnaces and their walls and arches tower across the open space. They are overgrown, access prevented by the health and safety conscious installation of protective fencing, uninterpreted beyond a single badly damaged display board but there. They start, four storeys tall, and then they go on and on. A murder of crows circle, swoop from putlog hole to putlog. These remains have not been homogenised nor repainted and repaired for tidy viewing by a tidy public. Amid the sprouting buddleia and whirling birds there is an air of the past's hellscape. Out there at the edge of consciousness. Perhaps. The whole edifice is certainly unexpected and if Geraint Talfan's Cyfarthfa Foundation gets its funding one of the elevated glass-sided walkways will reach just here from the hillside castle.

SOUTH TO THE MARKET

The Latter Day Saints are as gleaming white here as they are everywhere else. I love the assured silence these churches radiate. To check out the view and to engage in yet

Church of Latter Day Saints

another spot of psychogeographic mysticism we divert uphill briefly to access the terraces of Cyfarthfa Retail Park, sitting largely on the top of what was once the great gleaming white cinder tip of the blast furnaces. We visit the more northerly and smaller section where branches of B&Q and Pets R Us have been erected over what was once Crawshay's complex of coke ovens. Before the deep piling and ground-works necessary for contemporary retail, Glamorgan-Gwent Archaeological Trust were allowed to dig. They uncovered slices of the past that Merthyr keeps on obliterating. They've erected an interpretive signboard at the car park's southern end showing maps past and present and describing what they found. Through the trees the blue clock face of Pandy Farm sits visible below the fake battlements of leaking Cyfarthfa Castle itself.

Back downhill the path bends through housing where the streets, in the days of Merthyr's yore, were mostly named after English kings but in their twenty-first century replacements are called Llwyn Dic Penderyn and Heol S.O. Davies cele-brating the town's more radical sons.

We emerge at O'Sullivan's Celtic Bar, a pub that majors on pride, promotion and craic and has plastered its outsides with giant pictures of marauding Celtic armies offering three drinks for a fiver all night. Inflation slows in these parts. The Celt, built in 1795 as the Three Horse Shoes was back then a meeting place for radicals and central to the uprising.

Just beyond Merthyr Tydfil Fire Station a path at the top of the College Car Park leads to a preserved engine house, part of Crawshay's Cyfarthfa iron works extension at Ynys Fach. The new college is built across the site with the iron works rail sidings underneath the car park. The preserved structure is stuffed into a tiny gap back of the now looming college and strapped around with chain fence and a locked gate. Its internal reinterpretation of the site awaits rays of light and flows of cash, I guess.

Back out in the car park the pedestrian bridge over the river and into the heart of Merthyr Market has a Banksy style piece of street art tagged RVK at its entrance. It's a child holding the word CENSORED in revolutionary red. How the young world is. A market hall has occupied this spot for a long time. The current incarnation adds high street stores to market stalls and joins the complex with escalators and stairs. On the first floor, trying to find the way out I ask an aproned bakery stall holder and am told "down them stairs and then follow yourself back out". Clear as day but I know what he means. There are two more of Merthyr's boxers standing on plinths here. 'The People's Champion' Howard Winstone Featherweight Champion of the World 1968 and then round the corner the Matchstick Man, tiny Johnny Owen, bantamweight champion. He was knocked out when he fought Mexican Lupe Pintor in 1980. He never regained consciousness. He was 24. On his plinth outside Greggs his anorexic form forever frozen, his hooked nose slicing the air.

On the way back to the station a RVK's Banksyesque Boris makes a thumbs up. Above are the words, never truer than here in Merthyr – 'The Rich Will Stay Rich, The Poor Will Stay Poor'.

Johnny Owen,
the Matchstick Man

THE BEST WORKS OF FICTION
SET IN THE INDUSTRIAL SOUTH WALES VALLEYS

As these valleys John Briggs and I have been walking are covered as much by fiction as they are by maps I asked a number of prominent Welsh critics to name their top fives. The results throw up some common ground, few women and only one author who is still alive, Christopher Meredith. I'll make that two by adding Dai Smith's *The Crossing*. Read these volumes and you'll get the complete experience without visiting at all.

SAM ADAMS:
Shifts – Christopher Meredith
How Green was My Valley – Richard Llewellyn
Black Parade – Jack Jones
Times Like These – Gwyn Jones
Cwmardy – Lewis Jones

KATIE GRAMICH:
The Withered Root – Rhys Davies
Black Parade – Jack Jones
Oscar – Gwyn Thomas
The Small Mine – Menna Gallie
Shifts – Christopher Meredith

DARYL LEEWORTHY:
All Things Betray Thee – Gwyn Thomas
Jubilee Blues – Rhys Davies
The Alone to the Alone – Gwyn Thomas
The Full-Time Amateur – Ron Berry
The Red Hills – Rhys Davies

JOHN PIKOULIS:
This Bygone – Ron Berry
Cwmardy – Lewis Jones
Island of Apples – Glyn Jones
Black Parade – Jack Jones
Times Like These – Gwyn Jones

DAI SMITH:
All Things Betray Thee – Gwyn Thomas
A Time To Laugh – Rhys Davies
Cwmardy – Lewis Jones
The Dark Philosophers – Gwyn Thomas
Flame and Slag – Ron Berry

NOTES

ABERCYNON

1. *Aber* in Welsh means not only river mouth (as in, for example *Abertawe*, the Welsh name for Swansea) but also the place where rivers meet. In Aberdare it is where the Dare flows into the Cynon and here it is where the Cynon meets the Taff.
2. House prices rises in the whole of the Valleys appear to be on the up. Declared in 2022 as a hot spot. Price increases among Valley terraces have outstripped the rate for everywhere else in Wales.

ABERDARE

3. See endnote 1 above
4. St Elvan's Church, 1851, built by the Bute family, Pennant stone dressed with bath stone. Four-stage west tower and spire with an interior which John Newman, in an uncharacteristic moment of commendation, calls "a revelation…everything has been whitened, so that one feels momentarily as if one has stepped into a C17 Dutch painting of a church interior" – *The Buildings of Wales*, Penguin Books, 1995
5. Sometimes known as Daviestown.
6. Including for a few years a mixed gauge Vale of Neath Railway.

ABERFAN

7. Pit wheel removed from the grounds of Ysgol Rhyd y Grug. Wooden carving of a miner now bearing a few fungal blossoms by Chris Wood of Wood Art Wales, in Newport.
8. See www.dark-tourism.com which lists destinations from Albania to Zimbabwe.
9. Lewis, Huw, *To Hear The Skylark's Song – A Memoir* of *Aberfan*, Parthian Modern Wales Series, 2017.
10. Ron Davies, in 1997 Secretary of State for Wales, arranged for the Welsh Office to repay the capital sum taken – £150,000.
11. Davies, Walter Haydn, *Blithe Ones*, Alun Books, 1979. Long out of print but available on the second hand market. My copy cost £10 and came signed, inscribed with the words "to strive, to seek and not to yield" and with a review cutting and photo of the author taken from *Y Cymro*, March, 1981 folded into the pages.

BARGOED

12. The 'Bargod' you see on the occasional bilingual sign means 'boundary' but such usage been lost in the Anglo-Welsh gallop towards a common industrial future.
13. What was the great Lowry doing in the south Wales Valleys at the height of his fame? Visiting, it seems, with his patron, Monty Bloom, who came from Ebbw Vale and had been raised in the Rhondda.
14. 'O worship the Lord in the beauty of holiness' arcs above the organ. Below are two latter-day additions, a black and white cut out Welsh dragon and a yellow neon reading 'be kind'.
15. His name appears fifteen times. His nearest rivals are Idris Davies and Rhys Davies who manage twelve. Jack Jones manages ten.
16. "I was born in 1927 and I want to know why," was John Tripp's in his cups mantra, chanted so often that those around him became able to imitate him perfectly. He never found the answer. His blacksmith father went to America in 1929 seeking an escape from the prevalent depression and leaving the young JT to be brought up by his mother. On his father's return, success having eluded him, the family moved to Whitchurch in Cardiff, to a bungalow called Pendarves after the farm in Cornwall where the Tripp family had its origins. Despite his father's wishes to the contrary JT never took up blacksmithing but became a rumbustious poet instead. More walks in Trippland are detailed in the ramble around Taffs Well (see page 136). Tripp fans can find a lot more about their anti-hero in Tony Curtis' *The Meaning of Apricot Sponge – Selected Writings of John Tripp*, Parthian, 2010

CAERPHILLY

17. "The Start of a New Journey – More Services | New Trains | Better Stations - Coming your way"
18. The statue was sculpted by James Done. On a recent Red Nose day it was embellished with a plastic nose but this was stolen.
19. Carved by John Merrill out of wood from Powys Castle Estate.
20. In 1913 Caerphilly Co-operative Garden Village Society planned a development of 100 houses with institute, playing fields and a park. Only 8 were ever built. The land was sold for school development.
21. Not that nearby. The Elizabethan mansion of Llancaiach Fawr complete on set days with costumed history reinterpreters is halfway up the Rhymney Valley at Nelson.

22. The Van's example dates from 1583.
23. A pannier tanker 9480 which had arrived that morning pulling the works train.

GELLI

24. David Davies 1818-1890 born in Llandinam, Montgomeryshire. Industrialist, Liberal politician and the founder of the Ocean Coal Company and Barry Docks.
25. Closed in 2001 following a damning report by David Purchon. There were local fears of birth defects, rats and smells. "too wet, too windy and too close to nearby residents" was the official line.
26. Thorpe, Adam, *On Silbury Hill*, Little Toller, 2014, a chalkland memoir that I couldn't put down.
27. Coflein is the online database for the National Monuments Record of Wales (NMRW) – the national collection of information about the historic environment of Wales. The name is derived from the Welsh cof (memory) and lein (line). https://coflein.gov.uk/ – Search for 'Mynydd-y-Gelli'.

GELLIGAER

28. Torrance, Chris, 'Citrinas', *The Magic Door,* Test Centre, 2017.
29. Watkins, Alfred, *The Old Straight Track – Its Mounds, Beacons, Moats, Sites and Mark Stones*, Heritage Hunter, 2015. First published 1925.
30. John returns at a later date to attend eucharist and manages to view and photograph the stone and the stocks and the Morgan screen. It can be done.
31. Sir Arthur Evans, 1851-1941 – archaeologist and recreator of Aegean civilization at a fancifully reconstructed Knossos on Crete.
32. Named after the local land owner John Capel Hanbury rather than Gwladys' Capel.

PONTYPRIDD

33. Benches created by south Wales artist blacksmith Andrew Rowe's Dar Designs.
34. Taliesin James, son of Evan James (Ieuan ap Iago), composer of the lyrics for the National Anthem of Wales.
35. The Lido closed in 1991 and was reopened following considerable Lottery-funded refurbishment in 2015. The storms of February 2020 closed it again for more than a year. It reopened on May 1, 2021.

PORTH

36. Coal City.
37. John Leland, the antiquarian and traveller who toured Wales between 1536 and 1542.
38. Period posters and photographs of early steam rail operations are a feature of Valleys' rail stations – especially those at Caerphilly and Rhymney.
39. Known as America-Fâch, according to the WJEC (http://resource.download.wjec.co.uk.s3-eu-west-1.amazon-aws.com/vtc/2018-19/18-19_2-1/pdf/patterns-of-migration-welsh-context.pdf), because "In the 19th century, many of its residents had spent time living in the USA before returning to Wales".
40. Thomas, Gwyn, *Selected Short Stories*, Poetry Wales Press, 1984
41. Thomas, Gwyn, *All Things Betray Thee*, a novel from 1949. In the 2011 Library of Wales edition published by Parthian there is an introduction by Raymond Williams.

RHYMNEY

42. Although we'll need to forgive them, irritating though it may be, for mispronouncing *Rhymney* as *Rimney*, in order to rhyme with 'give me' as in 'oh what will you give me, say the sad bells of Rimney' American folk singers have taken this poem places. Yet they don't always mispronounce the word. John tells me that when he saw Roger McGuinn, the Byrds lead singer, in a solo concert at the Beaufort Theatre, Ebbw Vale in the early 2000s McGuinn pronounced Rhymney correctly. All is not lost.
43. *To Idris Davies* – Mike Jenkins, on the AmeriCymru website: https://americymru.net/americymru/blog/2069 /to-idris-davies-mike-jenkins
44. 'Also for their son Idris Davies (the poet) who died April 6, 1953 aged 48. He will never be forgotten.'
45. The estate was developed by Richard Johnson, the ironworks manager, to plans based on James Adams's proposed model village at Lowther in Cumbria of 1765.

TAFFS WELL

46. *Real Cardiff – The Flourishing City*, Seren, 2018: 'The Slow Erosion of John Tripp's Whitchurch'.
47. *Walking Cardiff,* Seren, 2019 page 205.

48. Cofiwch Dryweryn – Remember Tryweryn – a slogan of protest at the 1965 drowning of a Welsh valley in order to supply water for Liverpool. The original is on a derelict cottage wall just outside Llanrhystud. In recent years the slogan has been revived and has been used across Wales as an enduring protest against English rule and Westminster interference in Welsh affairs.
49. *The Englishman Who Went Up a Hill But Came Down a Mountain* by Christopher Monger and starring Hugh Grant, Tara Fitzgerald and Colm Meaney.
50. Gillham, Mary, *The Garth Countryside,* Lazy Cat Publishing, 1999.
51. Home of Wales' only thermal spring.
52. Meier, Peg, *Bring Warm Clothes – letters and photos from Minnesota's Past*, Minneapolis Tribune.
53. The Rhys Davies Trust was a registered charity which supported Welsh literary projects. It was wound up at the end of 2021.

TONYPANDY

54. The Rhondda Tramways Company was set up in 1904. It ultimately connected Treherbert to Pontypridd with a branch to Maerdy and to one on to Blaenrhondda. In 1920 motor coaches were introduced on a new route along Clydach Vale. The beginning of the end. Over the ensuing decade trams were steadily replaced by buses and all tram operation ceased in 1934.
55. Davies, Rhys, *A Time To Laugh,* Library of Wales, 2015. Originally published 1937.
56. Tommy Farr's son was Gary Farr who led the cult 60s r&b band, Gary Farr and the T-Bones. The family had moved to Sussex by this time (1965). It would be great to report that the band had played a seminal gig at Judge's Hall but, so far, I've found no reference to that.
57. Davies, Rhys, *Print of a Hare's Foot – An Autobiographical Beginning,* first published in 1969 currently available, 1998, from Seren. With a considerable amount of exaggeration along with some sheer invention this is not the most accurate of recollections. It is nonetheless a good read.

TREHERBERT

58. Tower went the way of all the rest in 2008. Last deep pit gone, a history finished.
59. Osmond, John (ed), *Futures for the Heads of the Valleys*, Institute of Welsh Affairs, 2008
60. Known locally as the Hook and Eye after its unusual winding gear. Drawings of the pit in the 1940s by Isabel Alexander are included in the Parthian expanded reprint of B.L. Coombes, *Miner's Day*, 2021
61. Coleg Harlech – 1927-2017 Workers' Educational Association mature student residential college offering two-year diplomas validated by the University of Wales to qualifying students from Wales.

YSTRAD MYNACH

62. Glastonselfy – named in memory of cancer sufferer Leanne Self who died in 2015.

MERTHYR TYDFIL

63. England, Joe, *Merthyr – The Crucible Of Modern Wales,* Parthian Modern Wales series, 2017.
64. *Anonymous Bosch*, Poetry by Mike Jenkins, Images by Dave Lewis, Culture Matters, 2021.
65. Moved twice before and now settled here this Merthyr listed landmark was a gift to the people at the time of Merthyr's incorporation as a County Borough in 1906. It was funded by Lord Merthyr, Sir W.T. Lewis. It's dedicated to his grandparents, Robert and Lucy Thomas. Lucy was known as the mother of the Welsh steam coal trade, an illiterate widow who worked on as a coal owner at her pits in nearby Troed-y-Rhiw long after her husband's death in 1833.
66. Gustavius Payne's work can be viewed at https://www.guspayne.com/
67. The Tiger gets a few mentions in Jack Jones' *Bidden To the Feast* (1938) and a few more in Glyn Jones' *The Island of Apples* (1965). This shows the power of research as The Tiger was renamed The Imperial in 1861.
68. Currently subject to regeneration as offices.
69. *Anonymous Bosch*, Poetry by Mike Jenkins, Images by Dave Lewis, Culture Matters, 2021.
70. A fourth, a life size real shorts wearing mannequin of Mike Tyson stands outside the premises of ABC Exchange & Mart House Clearance Specialists. When I ask if the mannequin ever gets stolen the owner the owner tells me "Don't be daft, butt, this is Merthyr".
71. 'Myfanwy' is a tune known by almost all Welsh people today. It was composed by Parry and published in 1875. The words either came from a poem by Richard Davies or from a Davies restructuring of the words a poem written by Thomas Walter Price. Merthyr author Jack Jones further muddies the water in his fictionalising of the story of composition in his novel *Off To Philadelphia In The Morning* (1951).
72. Stephens, Meic, *The Oxford Companion To The Literature Of Wales,* OUP, 1986.

WORKS CONSULTED

GENERAL

Curtis, Tony, Ed, *The Meaning of Apricot Sponge – Selected Writings of John Tripp*, Parthian, 2010

Cooke, R A, *Gazetteer of the Coal Mines of South Wales & Monmouthshire From 1854*, Lightmoor Press, 2018

Coombes, B.L., *These Poor Hands – the autobiography of a miner working in south Wales*, UWP, 2002

Davies, Idris, *The Collected Poems Of Idris Davies*, Gwasg Gomer, 1972

Davies, John, *The Making Of Wales*, Sutton, 1996

Davies, John, *A History of Wales*, Allen Lane, 1993

Dicks, Brian, *Portrait of Cardiff and its Valleys*, Hale, 1984

Gaulde, Enid, *Cruel Habitations – A History of Working-Class Housing 1780-1918*, George Allen & Unwin, 1974

Hall, Mike, *Lost Railways of South Wales*, Countryside Books, 2009

Hodge, John, *Barry – Its Railway & Port*, Pen Sword, 2018

Kidner, R.W., *The Rhymney Railway,* The Oakwood Press, 1995

Lewis, E D, *The Rhondda Valleys*, University College Cardiff Press, 1958

Lowe, J.B., *Welsh Industrial Workers Housing 1775-1875*, National Museum of Wales, 1977

Lowe, J.B., *Welsh Country Workers Housing 1775-1875*, National Museum of Wales, 1985

Minchinton, W. E. (editor) *Industrial South Wales 1750-1914 Essays in Welsh Economic History,* Frank Cass, 1969

Morgan, Prys, *Writers of Wales Iolo Morganwg*, University of Wales Press, 1975

Page, James, *Rails In The Valleys*, Guild Publishing, 1989

Parker, Mike and Whitfield, Paul, *Wales The Rough Guide*, The Rough Guides, 1994

Paxman, Jeremy, *Black Gold – The History of How Coal Made Britain*, William Collins, 2021

Pride, Emrys, *Rhondda My Valley Brave*, Starling Press, 1975

Rowson, Stephen & Wright, Ian L., *The Glamorganshire & Aberdare Canals*, two vols, Black Dwarf, 2004

Smith, Dai, *The Crossing*, Parthian, 2020

Smith, Dai, *Wales! Wales?*, George Allen and Unwin, 1984

Smith, David (editor), *A People and a Proletariat – Essays in the History of Wales 1780-1980*, Pluto Press, 1980

Smith, Ewart, *Upper Rhymney Valley Through Time*, Amberley Publishing, 2010

Stephens, Meic (editor), *The Oxford Companion To The Literature Of Wales,* OUP, 1986

Swidenbank, David & Seward, Alun, *Rhondda Collieries Through Time*, Amberley Publishing, 2013

Thomas, Erin Ann, *Coal in Our Veins,* University Press of Colorado, 2012

Torrance, Chris, *The Magic Door,* Test Centre, 2017

Vinter, Jeff, *The Taff Trail Official Guidebook*, Alan Sutton, 1993

Watkins, Alfred, *The Old Straight Track – Its Mounds, Beacons, Moats, Sites and Mark Stones*, Heritage Hunter, 2015. First published 1925

Williams, Gwyn A., *When Was Wales*, Black Raven Press, 1985

Williams, Raymond, *The Welsh Industrial Novel*, University College Cardiff Press, 1978

ABERCYNON

Evans, George Ewart, *The Strength of the Hills – An Autobiography*, Faber, 1983

Williams, Gareth, Ask *The Fellows Who Cut The Coal – George Ewart Evans of Abercynon 1909-1988,* Keelin Publications, 2017

ABERDARE

Cynon Valley History Society, *Cynon Coal – History of a Mining Valley,* Cynon Valley History Society, 2001

Evans, Geoffrey, *Aberdare Park – A Guide and Short History*, The Friends of Aberdare Park, 2018

Lewis, Alun, *Collected Poems*, Seren, 1994

Rowson, Stephen and Wright, Ian L., *The Glamorganshire And Aberdare Canals Vol 1*, Black Dwarf Publications, 2001

ABERFAN

Gillham, Mary and others, *A Guide To The Historic Taff Valley From Quakers' Yard To Aberfan*, Merthyr Tydfil and District Naturalists' Society, 1979

Lewis, Huw, *To Hear The Skylark's Song – A Memoir*, Parthian Modern Wales, 2017

Madgwick, Gaynor, *Aberfan – The Story of Survival, Love and Community in One of Britain's Worst Disasters*, Y Lolfa, 2016

McLean, Iain & Johnes, Martin, *Aberfan – Government and Disaster*, Welsh Academic Press, 2000

Sheers, Owen, *The Green Hollow*, Faber, 2018

Walsh, Louise, *Black River – A Novel of the Aberfan Disaster 1966*, Gwasg Carreg Gwalch, 2016

Wroe, Jo Browning, *A Terrible Kindness,* Faber, 2022

BARGOED

Gelligaer Historical Society, *Bargoed and Gilfach – a Local History,* MWL Print Group, 2011

CAERPHILLY

Lloyd, Henry, *History of Caerphilly – From The Earliest Period To The Present Time (1900)*, Kessinger Legacy Reprints, 2019

Mountford, E.R., *Caerphilly Works 1901-1964*, Roundhouse Books, 1965

Richards, H P, *A History of Caerphilly*, D Brown & Sons, 1975

Turner, Rick, *Discover Caerphilly Castle*, CADW, 2016.

GELLIGAER

Gelligaer Historical Society Newsletters 2006 – 2022 http://gelligaerhistoricalsociety.co.uk/publications/newsletters/

Gelligaer Local History Appreciation Society, *magazine Vols 1 to 4,* 2012 onwards

Saunders, E John, *The Gelligaer Story*, Gelligaer Urban District Council, 1959

MERTHYR TYDFIL

Clarke, T.E., *A Guide To Merthyr Tydfil*, J P Lewis, 1894

England, Joe, *Merthyr The Crucible Of Modern Wales 1760-1912*, Parthian, 2017

Gross, Joseph, *A Brief History of Merthyr Tydfil,* Starling Press, 1980

Hayman, Richard, *Working Iron in Merthyr Tydfil,* Merthyr Tydfil Heritage Trust, 1989

Jenkins, Mike, (with Dave Lewis) *Anonymous Bosch*, Culture Matters, 2021

Llywelyn, Malcolm, *Merthyr Tydfil – Places Make History*, Llyfrau Brynach, 2019

Perkins, John and others, *The Historic Taf Valleys Vol Three – from the Taf confluence at Cefn-Coed-y-Cymmer to Aberfan*, Merthyr Tydfil and District Naturalists' Society, 1986

Trezise, Rachel, *Dial M For Merthyr*, Parthian, 2007
Cyfarthfa Castle Museum & Art Gallery Guide Book, Merthyr Tydfil Leisure Trust, 2021

PONTYPRIDD

ap Nicholas, Islwyn, *A Welsh Heretic – Dr William Price, Llantrisant*, The Ffynnon Press, 1973
Jones, Keith, *Bunch of Grapes – An Illustrated History*, Bunch of Grapes, 2012
Large, Robert, *Doctor Griffiths' Tramroad And Canal*, Pontypridd Museum, 2010
Powell, Don, *Victorian Pontypridd and its Villages*, Merton Priory Press, 1996
Rees, David James, *Pontypridd South Past & Present*, Starling Press, 1983
Richards, Alun, *Dai Country*, Parthian Library of Wales, originally published 1973
Seward, Alun & Swidenbank, David, *Pontypridd History Tour,* Amberley Publishing, 2014
Smith, Dai and Stephens, Meic (editors), *A Community And Its University – Glamorgan 1913-2003*, University of Wales Press, 2003

PORTH

Bacchetta, Aldo & Rudd, Glyn, *Porth – Gateway to the Rhondda*, Tempus, 2000
Thomas, Gwyn, *A Welsh Eye*, Hutchinson, 2007
Thomas, Gwyn, *Selected Short Stories*, Poetry Wales Press, 1984

RHYMNEY

Jones, Thomas, *Rhymney Memories*, Gwasg Gomer, 1970
Lawrence, Ray, *A Brief History of the Rhymney Iron Works*, Welsh Mining Books, 2016

TAFFS WELL

Gillham, Mary E., *The Garth Countryside – A Natural History,* Lazy Cat Publishing, 1999

TONYPANDY

Davies, Rhys, *Print Of A Hare's Foot*, Seren, 1998
Evans, Gwyn & Maddox, David, *The Tonypandy Riots 1910-1911*, University of Plymouth Press, 2010
Smith, Dai, *In The Frame – Memory in Society 1910 to 2019*, Parthian, 2010

TREHERBERT

Berry, Ron, *Flame and Slag*, Library of Wales, Parthian Books, 2012
Coombes, B.L., *Miner's Day* reprint including an extensive selection of the images of Isabel Alexander, Parthian, 2021
Cameron, Sean James, *Then & Now Rhondda – From Cwmparc to Blaencwm*, Tempus, 2001
Wakelin, Peter, *Charles Burton Painting Still*, Sansom & Company, 2019

TROED Y RHIW

Davies, Walter Haydn, *Blithe Ones*, Alun books, 1979

YSTRAD MYNACH

Griffiths, Maldwyn & Herold, Richard, *Old Ystrad Mynach including Hengoed, Cefn Hengoed and Maesycwmmer in Photographs*, Old Bakehouse Publications, 2001
Salway, Gareth, *Penallta Colliery – An Illustrated History 1901-1991*, Groundwork Caerphilly, 1993

MAPS

Alan Godfrey's reprints of old OS maps from1890s to the 1920s cover a good deal of the valleys. https://www.alangodfreymaps.co.uk/

Ordnance Survey contemporary mapping for the whole of the UK including both free and paid for content
https://osmaps.ordnancesurvey.co.uk/

Coflein – the online database for the National Monuments Record of Wales (NMRW) - the national collection of information about the historic environment of Wales. The name is derived from the Welsh cof (memory) and lein (line). Coflein contains details of many thousands of archaeological sites, monuments, buildings and maritime sites in Wales, together with an index to the drawings, manuscripts and photographs held in the NMRW archive collections. https://coflein.gov.uk/en/

CADW – is the Welsh Government's historic environment service. Their web site includes detailed mapping for listed locations.
https://cadw.gov.wales/

THANKS AND ACKNOWLEDGEMENTS

Sue read the script, more than once, and made many useful suggestions. She also accompanied the two of us on a few occasions and helped with the many fill-in visits necessary in the creation of a useable walk. Mick at Seren got excited again by the idea, sourced the finance and saw the project through. John Briggs with his caravanette (no longer a Mazda Bongo but now something much more modern although still with all its controls labelled in Japanese script) returned to our routes on many occasions to get just the right shot.

Conversations were had with local historians, literary critics, valley residents, poets, and people simply bumped into on the valley streets. In particular I'd like to thank Lyn Date, Don Brooks, Rachel Fenner, Dean Hopkins, Mike Jenkins, Dr Daryl Leeworthy, John Osmond, Ross Perriman, Teresa Rees and Craig Thomas of JJ castings Ltd, Stephen Ryan, and Professor Dai Smith.

PETER FINCH

Peter Finch is a poet, performer, author, psychogeographer and literary entrepreneur living in Cardiff. He has been a publisher, bookseller, event organiser, literary agent and literary promoter.

Poetry from his twenty or so books and pamphlets has been assembled in a two volume *Collected Poems*, edited by Andrew Taylor and published by Seren in 2022. His 2013 *Edging The Estuary,* the story of where Wales becomes England has recently been reprinted. His *The Roots of Rock From Cardiff To Mississippi And Back* appeared from Seren in 2016. *Edging The City*, a walk around the capital's border, was published in 2022.

He edits Seren's Real series of alternative handbooks, literary rambles and guides to Britain's conurbations. His own *Real Cardiff* (in four volumes) and *Real Wales* have appeared in this series.

"Peter Finch is a fine psychogeographer, a consummate chronicler of place both literal and ethereal, able to chop words with gleeful precision.... *Real Wales* is a reminder that he who first cooked up the concept remains its sharpest protagonist." – **Mike Parker** in *New Welsh Review*

www.peterfinch.co.uk

JOHN BRIGGS

John Briggs is an American photographer from Minnesota who has lived in south Wales since the 1970s. He is the author of three books published by Seren, documenting the changes that have taken place in Cardiff and Newport over the past four decades. He continues to photograph in both cities digitally and with film. Briggs has also previously worked extensively with Peter Finch photographing authors and literary events for Academi/Literature Wales.

In addition to published works, his images have been exhibited widely in Cardiff and Newport: Butetown History and Arts Centre, Pier Head Building Futures Gallery, Norwegian Church Arts Centre and St. David's Hall gallery among others. His photographs have featured recently in the BBC documentary 'Dock of the Bay' and his author portraits for the IWA are in the collection of the National Library of Wales in Aberystwyth.

Published works:

The Pubs of Newport, Handpost Books, 1997
Before the Deluge, Seren, 2002
Taken in Time, Seren, 2005
Newportrait, Seren, 2009
25/25 Vision – Welsh Horizons Across 50 Years, IWA, 2012.

Some of his photographs can be viewed at https://www.flickr.com/photos/jbsees60/sets/